Legal Almanac Series No. 33

THE LAW OF INHERITANCE

In All Fifty States

FOURTH EDITION

by EUGENE M. WYPYSKI, LL.B.
Member of the New York Bar

General Editor
Irving J. Sloan

1984
Oceana Publications, Inc.
London • Rome • New York

Library of Congress Catalog Card Number: 76-40542

International Standard Book Number (ISBN): 0-379-11106-3

The Legal Almanac Series brings you the law on various subjects in non-technical language. These books do not take the place of your attorney's advice, but they can introduce you to your legal rights and responsibilities.

Manufactured in the United States of America

Dedicated to

M.C.W.

et al.

TABLE OF CONTENTS

CHARTS

FOREWORD

It is a law of nature for people to be concerned about themselves, their personal wealth and worldly goods, irrespective of the size of their estate.

Thus, it is important to have authoritative information about the law of descent and distribution as it affects the right of inheritance.

The able author of this manual has made an exhaustive study of the statute laws of the several states resulting in an accurate, dependable and detailed compilation of the definitive law covering every phase of this important topic of law.

Among the textual subject matter included is community property, surviving spouse as heir, rights of children whether natural, adopted, illegitimate or posthumus, election against will, and rights of aliens. All matter is tabulated in concise form and provisions of the law are supported by cited statute references. His factual statements and conclusions are expressed in clear, frank language.

The aim of the following pages is to present a comprehensive view of the salient features of the law of descent and distribution as of today.

The lay user is cautioned to consult an attorney for further legal interpretation and advice prior to starting any action or Surrogate proceedings.

The book should serve as a dependable reference manual to attorney and laymen alike, for it gives the essential answers regarding the law of descent and distribution for all jurisdictions of these United States.

Lawrence H. Schmehl, *Librarian*
New York County Lawyers' Association

Chapter 1

PROPERTY SUBJECT TO INHERITANCE

INTRODUCTION

Whenever a person dies, we are always sure to find long lost relatives coming from near and far to claim a share of the estate. Perhaps the person died leaving a Will mentioning particular relatives, or the person may have died without a Will. In either case, the property which was owned will be transmitted to those entitled to inherit at the time of death.

There are various methods by which property may be transmitted on the death of the owner. The most important methods are by Will or by Intestate Succession. A Will is the legal declaration of a person's intent to be performed after death. Intestate Succession, sometimes called descent and distribution, is the transmission of property by operation of law.

When a person dies leaving a Will, the person dies testate; if the person does not leave a Will, the person dies intestate. An intestate share, therefore, is that share inherited from the estate of one who dies without having left a Will.

The right to inherit is not a natural right but one provided for by law. When a person dies intestate, the law provides who shall share in the estate. Such laws are based on principles of public policy and dispose of the estate as it is presumed the decedent would have done, based on natural love and affection.

HISTORY AND BACKGROUND—The English common law of inheritance was originally founded on the feudal canons of descent. Under the feudal canons real property passed to the eldest male son in preference to other children and to the male child over the female. The rules tended to disregard blood relationships in preference to promoting the accumulation of lands in the hands of a few, thereby conserving the splendor and influence of leading families.

The English common law only provided for the descent of real property. The rules for distribution of personal property were based on the Roman or Civil Law. Under this system succession was based on the family-blood relationship, rather than on succession to a select class or group. All children, as well as ancestors, of the decedent were capable of inheriting under the Civil law.

The present American law is based on both the Civil law and English common law. The early feudal canons of primogeniture and preference of male over female children were inconsistent with our fundamental political conceptions and hence never adopted. The Civil law system of distribution has influenced the American law particularly in the regions where the French and Spanish law were once in force.

Under our present statutes in some states, a distinction is sometimes drawn between descent and distribution. The term descent is usually applied to the passing of real property to the heirs of the deceased, while the term distribution applies to personal property which passes to the next-of-kin. In most states all real and personal property are grouped together, and the estate is then distributed according to law. It is important, where a distinction is drawn, to ascertain to which class a person belongs, i.e., whether he is entitled to the real property or personal property, because the debts of the deceased and the expenses of administration of the estate are usually paid first out of the personal property.

WHAT PROPERTY PASSES—All property which the deceased possessed or in which he had any interest at the time of his death becomes part of his estate. This would include all real estate, cash, securities, personal belongings, interest in a business, debts which were owed the deceased, and anything else of a tangible or intangible nature which is of value.

Certain property is not included in the general assets of the estate. An insurance policy payable to a named beneficiary and not to the person's estate is not an asset. United States Bonds held in the name of one person payable on death to another do not become part of the estate. If property is owned by two persons, as joint tenants with the right of survivorship, it will pass to the survivor by operation of law. Where an exemption is allowed the widow and surviving children, the exempt property is set aside and is not distributed as part of the estate.

All real estate and other real property interests which the decedent owned at his death descends according to the law of the place where is is located. All personal property is distributed according to the law of the place where the deceased was domiciled. The place of his death is not controlling, but rather where his permanent home was located. It is possible, therefore, that the law of many states might control the administration of one estate.

and personal property concerns the time when title to the property passes to those who will inherit. The right or title to real property passes immediately on the death of the decedent to heirs entitled to inherit, whereas the right and title to personal property passes to the administrator of the estate to be distributed to those entitled to inherit.

Although a person leaves a Will, it does not mean that only the legatees mentioned will inherit. In many states it is impossible to cut off a surviving spouse. The state laws provide for certain allowances that a wife may take, even though not so provided for in the Will. Another instance is the case of children; in some states a child may receive a share of the estate although not specifically mentioned in a Will. The above cases will be discussed more fully in chapters 3 and 4.

Where the deceased left a Will and property which he owned at the time of his death was not included in it, or he failed to have a residuary clause, or where the residuary clause lapses he may die partially intestate. In a situation where property is Willed to Aunt Nellie "if she be alive at the time of my death," and as a fact she does not survive the decedent, and no alternative bequest is made, nor a residuary clause included, the property does not pass under the Will.

In any situation where property does not, or cannot pass under a Will, it becomes part of the decedent's estate to descend and be distributed according to the laws of inheritance.

There are instances where the Will may prove to be invalid because of the testator's lack of capacity. The testator may have been insane or the Will may not have been properly signed or witnessed. In such cases the decedent will be considered as having died without a Will.

LIABILITY FOR DEBTS OF THE DECEDENT—Under the common law, debts owed by the decedent were paid out of the personal property assets alone. All debts had to be discharged by the administrator of the estate before the person entitled to any personal property could inherit. Under our present law all property of the estate is charged with the decedent's debts, except property which is specifically exempt by statute. Real property is usually charged only after the personal property is entirely exhausted. Anyone entitled to inherit is liable for the decedent's debts only to the extent of the property which he inherits. He cannot be charged with debts which exceed the value of his inheritance.

Chapter 2

PERSONS ENTITLED TO INHERIT

IN GENERAL

At the present time a distinction is generally no longer made between heirs and next-of-kin. Real property at one time descended only to heirs who took by direct line of blood. Personal property passed to the next-of-kin, meaning those in a degree of blood relationship to the decedent. Though sometimes referred to as heirs, a husband and wife are related to each other by affinity.

Each state has specific statutes enumerating the persons entitled to inherit from one who dies without leaving a will.

SPOUSE — The right of a surviving husband or wife to share in the estate of a deceased spouse is recognized in all states. The interest or amount received may be dependent on the number of children or descendants who survive or if none, whether or not parents, brothers, sisters or their children survived the decedent. In all cases, the spouse is usually entitled to some share of the decedent's property, whether or not he was survived by anyone else.

LINEAL AND COLLATERAL KINDRED—Descent can be either lineal or collateral. A degree of descent is the term used to denote the closeness of relationship to the decedent, each step in the line of descent being considered one degree. Lineal descent is one in the direct or blood line of the decedent; for example, from father to son, or grandfather to grandson, or from son to father or grandfather. Descent to collateral relatives, as from brother to sister or cousin to cousin, is called collateral descent. Lineal descent can be either downward to descendant or upward to ancestors.

LINEAL DESCENDANTS—Children and descendants are usually preferred in inheritance of the decedent's estate; however, the statutes usually provide that the children's inheritance in the estate is subject to the rights of the decedent's spouse. The property which passes to the children and descendants, as a class, is usually divided into as many shares as there are children and deceased children survived by issue. Each child takes one share and the issue of deceased children share in the estate to the same extent as their ancestor would have shared if he had survived. When the law speaks of children and descendants or issue or representatives, it means descendants in a direct or lineal descent and therefore includes grandchildren and great-grandchildren.

LINEAL ANCESTORS—The common law canon which did not permit real property to lineally ascend was never recognized by American law. The statutes usually provide that parents may inherit in certain cases; ancestors do not usually inherit when the decedent leaves children or descendants surviving. Parents sometimes inherit only in the absence of a surviving spouse, brothers or sisters. In New York the surviving spouse inherits the estate up to a specified sum, and the excess is divided between the spouse and parents or surviving parent, when the decedent is not survived by children or descendants.

COLLATERALS—Inheritance by collateral kindred is usually dependent on whether or not the spouse or parents survive the decedent. Collateral kindred do not inherit when children or descendants survive the decedent. Where property passes to brothers and sisters, and their children or descendants, the estate is divided into as many shares as there are brothers and sisters and deceased brothers and sisters survived by children. The descendants of deceased brothers and sisters take the share their ancestor would have taken if alive. Inheritance by representing a deceased ancestor among collaterals, does not usually go beyond children of brothers and sisters.

Brothers, sisters and descendants of deceased brothers and sisters are usually the only collaterals specifically mentioned in the statutes. The inheritance right of collaterals more remote from the decedent, is usually provided for by a general clause to the effect that the estate passes to "next-of-kin in equal degree."

DEGREES OF KINDRED—Where there are none of the persons enumerated by the inheritance laws, kindred in nearest degree to the decedent inherit to the exclusion of those of a more remote degree. A degree denotes the distance from one person to another in the lines of kindred. Degrees of kindred are computed according to two methods: the civil law method and the common law method. By the civil law method degrees are determined by counting from the decedent up to the common ancestor and then down to the claimant; each step or degree in both the ascending and descending lines is considered one degree. Under the Civil law method, therefore, an uncle is related to the decedent in the third degree, i.e., in the ascending line from the decedent to his parent (one degree); then to the grandparent (second degree) then descending to the grandparents' child, i.e., the decedent's uncle (third degree).

DECEDENT → PARENT → GRANDPARENT
↓
UNCLE

According to the common law method, the rule is to begin counting from the common ancestor downward to the claimant. The distinction between the two methods is that the steps counted up to the common ancestor are degrees under the civil law method, and not under the common law method. Except in a few states where the common law rule is specifically provided for in the computation of kindred, most states provide for the civil law method.

The following illustrates various degrees of relationship under the civil law scheme:

Degree	Relationship to Decedent
First	Parents, children
Second	Grandparents, brothers and sisters
Third	Great-grandparents, uncles, aunts, nephews and nieces
Fourth	Great-great-grandparents, great-uncles, great-aunts, first cousins

MURDER OF THE DECEDENT—At common law a murderer could not inherit from his victim. This was true whether the victim died with or without a Will. The rule is based on the theory that one cannot benefit from his own wrong.

Under our present law, some states provide specifically for this situation, while others have interpreted the common law rule. Where there is no specific statute, some states provide that the slayer does not take his share while other states hold to the contrary.

A majority of the states have statutes denying an inheritance from a victim to a murderer. The slayer must be convicted, however, as a mere accusation or verdict of a coroner's jury is not sufficient.

Usually the statute provides that the property which would have been inherited by the slayer passes as part of the estate of the victim, to the same extent as if the slayer predeceased the victim. For the purpose of inheritance from the victim, the slayer is considered civilly dead.

SIMULTANEOUS DEATH — Where two persons die in a common accident or disaster, it is often very difficult, if not impossible, to ascertain which person died first. This is important where the deceased persons are closely related, and part or all of the estate would go to one or the other. For example, if a husband and wife died together, and under the laws of inheritance the spouse would take all, if the husband died first the estate would go to the wife and then to her heirs, and the reverse if the wife died first.

In forty six of the states, the Uniform Simultaneous Death Act has been passed. This act provides that where it cannot be ascertained which of two persons died first, the estate of each will be treated as if he survived the other. In other words, the husband's estate would pass to his heirs, as if he lived one instant longer than his wife, and the wife's estate would pass to her heirs as if she lived one instant longer than her husband.

The Uniform Simultaneous Death Act provides that where it cannot be ascertained which of two persons died first, the estate of each will be treated as if he survived the other. In other words, the husband's estate would pass to his heirs, as if he lived one instant longer than his wife, and the wife's estate would pass to her heirs as if she lived one instant longer than her husband.

Where property is held jointly and there is no sufficient evidence that the owners have died otherwise than simultaneously, the property is distributed one-half as if one had survived and one-half as if the other had survived.

The Uniform Simultaneous Death Act has been adopted by all states except Alaska, Louisiana, Montana and Ohio. It should be noted, however, that the four states have adopted individual statutes disigned to deal with this special situation.

The Uniform Probate Code requires that the heir survive the decedent for 120 hours. "Any person who fails to survive the decedent by 120 hours is deemed to have predeceased the decedent for purposes of homestead allowance, exempt property and intestate succession, and the decedent's heirs are determined accordingly" (U.P.C. §2-104).

ESCHEAT — Where there is no person qualified to take the decedent's property under the laws of inheritance, then the property escheats, i.e., passes to the state. In most states, the laws provide for inheritance by heirs although their relationship to the decedent is remote. Of course, the possibility of escheat can be prevented by the execution of a Will.

Chapter 3

RIGHTS OF SURVIVING SPOUSE

DOWER AND CURTESY GENERALLY—At common law the surviving spouse had a right of dower or curtesy in the real property of the deceased spouse. The surviving wife's dower right consisted of a one-third interest for life in all the real property owned by the husband during his life. Curtesy was the right of the husband to a life estate in all of the deceased wife's real property. The life estate which is taken consists of the use and enjoyment of real property for the duration of the recipient's life, including all rents and profits which are derived from the land. This interest can usually be sold or assigned subject always to termination on the death of the original recipient.

Dower and curtesy attach to any property which the spouse owned at any time during the marriage, whether or not such property was conveyed by deed. The right is usually barred, however, where both husband and wife join in a conveyance of the property.

a. Dower-Under our present statutes many variations of the common law right of dower exist. In some states the right has been completely abolished, while in others statutory substitutions or modifications have been enacted. Certain requirements are necessary for a widow to be entitled to dower, namely: (1) Lawful marriage; (2) The husband was possessed of an estate of inheritance in property, i.e., he owned a real property interest; and (3) The wife must survive the husband. Although the requirements are derived from common law, they have usually been incorporated in the statutes of those states which have retained the dower right.

Under certain circumstances the right of dower may be defeated. The wife can release her right by joining in the conveyance of the property by her husband or by a property settlement between the husband and wife. The right of dower is usually barred where the wife abandons her husband without just cause or is divorced because of her adultery or other misconduct. A condemnation proceeding, which is the lawful taking of property by the state or local government, usually bars dower. The dower right always terminates on the death of the widow.

b. Curtesy—The common law right of curtesy has been abolished either expressly or impliedly in a majority of the states. As a substitute many states provide an interest for the husband similar to the dower interest granted to the wife.

The common law requirements for curtesy are as follows: (1) Lawful marriage; (2) Wife owned an estate or interest in real property which could pass by inheritance; and (3) Birth of a child capable of inheriting. The requirements are historical and have been modified in most states, where any form of the curtesy interest exists.

Where the right of curtesy or dower has been abolished or is unknown, the survivor usually takes as an heir of the deceased spouse under the laws of inheritance.

The following will illustrate the rights of the surviving husband and wife in the real property of the deceased spouse. In the majority of cases, the interest which the surviving spouse takes is in addition to the rights of inheritance as an heir. In order to properly ascertain the complete rights of inheritance of the surviving spouse, it is necessary to read the following charts in connection with the succeeding section on the rights of the spouse as heir.

RIGHT OF DOWER, CURTESY AND STATUTORY SUBSTITUTIONS

ALABAMA	
Husband	Abolished (§2-113)
Wife	Abolished (§2-113)
ALASKA	
Husband	Abolished
Wife	Abolished
ARIZONA	
Husband	Abolished (§1-201)
Wife	Abolished (§1-201)
ARKANSAS	
Husband	Life estate in one-third of wife's real property and one-third of all personal property absolutely (§61-201,2)
Wife	Life estate in one-third of husband's real property and one-third of all personal property absolutely (§61-201,2)
CALIFORNIA	
Husband	None (Civil Code §5129)
Wife	None (Civil Code §5129)
COLORADO	
Husband	None (ch. 15-11-113)
Wife	Abolished (ch. 15-11-113)
CONNECTICUT	
Husband	None
Wife	None
DELAWARE	
Husband	Abolished (T.12 §511)
Wife	Abolished (T.12 §511)

FLORIDA	
Husband	Abolished (§732.111)
Wife	Abolished (§732.111)
GEORGIA	
Husband	None (§53-1-2)
Wife	Abolished (Laws of 1969)
HAWAII	
Husband	Life estate in one-third of wife's real property and one-third of all personal property absolutely. Rights must accrue prior to 7/1/77. (§533-16)
Wife	Life estate in one-third of husband's real property and one-third of all personal property absolutely. Rights must accrue prior to 7/1/77. (§533-16)
IDAHO	
Husband	Abolished (§32-914)
Wife	None (§32-914)
ILLINOIS	
Husband	Abolished (Probate Act §2-9)
Wife	Abolished (Probate Act §2-9)
INDIANA	
Husband	Abolished (§29-1-2-11)
Wife	Abolished (§29-1-2-11)
IOWA	
Husband	None
Wife	None
KANSAS	
Husband	One-half absolutely, of all wife's real property (§59-505)
Wife	One-half absolutely, of all husband's real property (§59-505)

KENTUCKY	
Husband	One-half of real property held at death plus life estate in one-third of real property held during marriage but not at time of death (§392.020)
Wife	One-half of real property held at death plus life estate in one-third of real property held during marriage but not at time of death (§392.020)
LOUISIANA	
Husband	None
Wife	None
MAINE	
Husband	Abolished (T.18-A, §2-113)
Wife	Abolished (T.18-A, §2-113)
MARYLAND	
Husband	Abolished (§3-202)
Wife	Abolished (§3-202)
MASSACHUSETTS	
Husband	Life estate in one-third of wife's real property (ch. 189 §1)
Wife	Life estate in one-third of husband's real property (ch. 189 §1)
MICHIGAN	
Husband	Abolished
Wife	Life estate in one-third husband's real property (§558.1)
MINNESOTA	
Husband	Abolished (§519.09)
Wife	Abolished (§519.09)
MISSISSIPPI	
Husband	Abolished (§93-3-5)
Wife	Abolished (§93-3-5)

MISSOURI	
Husband	Abolished (§474-110)
Wife	Abolished (§474-110)
MONTANA	
Husband	None (§72-2-701)
Wife	Abolished (§72-2-701)
NEBRASKA	
Husband	Abolished (§30-104)
Wife	Abolished (§30-104)
NEVADA	
Husband	Abolished (§123.020)
Wife	Abolished (§123.020)
NEW HAMPSHIRE	
Husband	Abolished (ch. 560 §3)
Wife	Abolished (ch. 560 §3)
NEW JERSEY	
Husband	Life estate in one-half real property acquired prior to May 28, 1980. (T.3B, c.28)
Wife	Life estate in one-half husband's real property acquired prior to May 28, 1980. (T.3B, c.28)
NEW MEXICO	
Husband	None (§45-2-13)
Wife	None (§45-2-13)
NEW YORK	
Husband	Abolished where wife dies after 8/31/30 (R.P.L. §189)
Wife	Abolished if married after 9/1/30 (R.P.L. §190)
NORTH CAROLINA	
Husband	Abolished (§29-4)
Wife	Abolished (§29-4)

NORTH DAKOTA	
Husband	None (§14-0709)
Wife	Abolished (§56-0102)
OHIO	
Husband	Life estate in one-third of wife's real property (§2103.02)
Wife	Life estate in one-third of husband's real property (§2103.02)
OKLAHOMA	
Husband	Abolished (T.84 §214)
Wife	Abolished (T.84 §214)
OREGON	
Husband	Abolished for surviving spouse who dies after 7/1/70 (§112.695)
Wife	Abolished for surviving spouse who dies after 7/1/70 (§112.695)
PENNSYLVANIA	
Husband	None
Wife	None
RHODE ISLAND	
Husband	Life estate in wife's real property (§33-25-2)
Wife	Life estate in husband's real property (§33-25-2)
SOUTH CAROLINA	
Husband	Abolished (§21-5 10)
Wife	Life estate in one-third of husband's real property (4S.C.37) (§21-5-720)
SOUTH DAKOTA	
Husband	Abolished (§29-1-3)
Wife	Abolished (§29-1-3)

TENNESSEE	
Husband	Abolished, unless vested before 4/1/77 (§31-202)
Wife	Abolished, unless vested prior to 4/1/77 (§31-202)
TEXAS	
Husband	None
Wife	None
UTAH	
Husband	Abolished (§75-2-113)
Wife	Abolished (§75-2-113)
VERMONT	
Husband	One-half of real property if issue of wife survives, or heir by adoption, if not then one-third of real property (T.14 §474)
Wife	One-half of real property if issue of husband survives, or heir by adoption, if not then one-third of real property (T.14 §461)
VIRGINIA	
Husband	Life estate in one-third of wife's real property (64.1-19)
Wife	Life estate in one-third of husband's real property (64.1-19)
WASHINGTON	
Husband	Abolished (§11.04, 060)
Wife	Abolished (§11.04, 060)
WEST VIRGINIA	
Husband	Life estate in one-third of wife's real property (c.43 art. 1 §1)
Wife	Life estate in one-third of husband's real property (c.43 art. 1 §1)

WISCONSIN

Husband	Life estate in one-third of property owned by wife at death (§861.03)
Wife	Life estate in one-third of property owned by husband at death (§861.03)

WYOMING

Husband	Life estate in one-third of property owned by wife at death (§861.03)
Wife	Life estate in one-third of property owned by husband at death (§861.03)

SURVIVING SPOUSE AS HEIR - Dower and curtesy or the statutory equivalents thereof are property rights which grow out of the marital relation. On the death of a husband or wife, the property which forms the estate of the deceased descends or is distributed according to the laws of inheritance. In the states where the dower or curtesy exists all rights of inheritance are subject to such rights of the surviving spouse.

At common law, real estate did not descend to the surviving spouse, but only to the heirs of the deceased. The right to any real estate of the deceased existed only by virtue of the right of dower or curtesy. To a limited extent, the surviving spouse shared in the personal property.

The surviving spouse in many states has a right of inheritance in the estate of the deceased in addition to any dower or curtesy right. The right of inheritance is statutory as the spouse is not strictly speaking, the heir or next of kin of the decedent. The amount or share which the spouse takes is usually dependent on the number of children or their descendants who survive and also on whether or not the deceased was survived by parents, brothers or sisters or their descendants.

Some jurisdictions provide for an inheritance as an alternative to dower or curtesy, the spouse being required to elect. Where dower and curtesy no longer exist, the spouse usually takes under the laws of inheritance, which provide for the descent and distribution of all real and personal property.

The question arises as to the distinction between the situation where the spouse receives dower or curtesy plus an interest in the estate under the laws of inheritance, and the case where only an interest under the laws of inheritance is taken and no right of dower or curtesy exists. The right of dower or curtesy is an interest in real property, which may be defeated or barred. This right cannot usually be defeated by the mere conveyance of the property by one spouse alone. It is an interest which is inchoate during the lifetime of both, and accrues absolutely on the death of the spouse. The right to take under the laws of inheritance, on the other hand, accrues on the death of the spouse, and only affects such property which was owned by the decedent at his death, subject to certain rights and liabilities as outlined by the statutes.

In the outline at the end of this chapter on the rights of the surviving spouse in the several states, it must be noted that the share taken under the laws of inheritance is usually in addition to any right of dower or curtesy, if such right exists, unless the statute provides that an election between the share must be made. Where the rights of the surviving spouse are dependent on the existence of issue or lineal descendants, the statutes usually construe the words to mean any children, grand-children, great-grand children and so down the line of direct lineal descendants.

COMMUNITY PROPERTY—In eight states, there exists a system of property ownership known as "community property". Under this system of law, the property acquired by the husband and wife, or by either of them during the marriage, otherwise than by specified ways, is community property. It is in effect in Arizona, California, Idaho, Louisiana, Nevada, New Mexico, Texas and Washington. Other states had enacted community property laws but the statutes were subsequently substantially abolished or declared unconstitutional.

The law of community property was derived from the Spanish and French civil law systems, and is not based on our Anglo-American common law system. Although the disposition of community property varies from state to state, the surviving spouse always inherits one-half of such property. In Texas the survivng spouse takes title to the entire community property, if there are no surviving children, and to one-half if the deceased spouse is survived by any children or other descendants. In Washington, the surviving spouse takes title to one-half of the community property while the remaining one-half is divided between the children and the surviving spouse.

Property owned by the husband and wife before marriage as well as property acquired by gift, devise, descent or in exchange for other separate property, is not community property of the husband and wife. The laws of inheritance in community property states usually provide separate rules of descent and distribution for community property and separately owned property.

HOMESTEAD—Legislatures, recognizing the family as the basic unit of our society, have enacted laws which protect the existence of the family home and provide allowances for the surviving spouse and children.

The dwelling house in which the family resides, together with customary appurtenances and incident land are usually referred to as the homestead. The important feature of the homestead law is the protection of property from the claims of creditors.

The husband is usually given the right to select the homestead, although the wife may be so empowered where the husband fails to do so. It may be selected from the property of either spouse, or from the common property of the marriage. In some states, however, a wife must consent to the selection of a homestead from her separate property.

In addition to protection from creditors, there are other important restrictions which protect the homestead. After the homestead has been declared, some states require that consent of both husband and wife is necessary before it can be abandoned; while in others no change can be made in the homestead limits without the consent of the other spouse.

The survivor has a vested interest in the homestead on the death of the husband or wife. The interest which the survivor takes may consist of absolute ownership or a right to use the property for life. In all cases, the interest taken is protected from creditors up to the amount set forth by statute. In community property states, where a homestead was not selected before the death of the decedent, the court will usually set aside a "probate homestead" for the benefit of the surviving spouse.

In addition, the survivor retains the right of homestead even though the decedent died with a Will which attempted to dispose of it. In such an instance the surviving spouse can elect against the Will and so take the homestead.

In states where the surviving spouse is entitled to dower or curtesy, the right of homestead is sometimes considered a part of the dower or curtesy interest, while in other states where the spouse takes as heir under the laws of inheritance, the homestead is in addition to any other share of the estate.

The following illustrates the limit of value and area of the homestead in the several states. A few states, such as Florida and Kansas, do not place a limit on the value of the homestead, although the acreage may be limited. In Kansas the statute defines a homestead as 160 acres of farming land, or of one acre lying within the limits of an incorporated city which is used as a residence at the time of one spouse's death. There are no homestead statutes in Connecticut, Delaware, District of Columbia, Maryland, New Jersey, Pennsylvania, and Rhode Island. Indiana allows urban homesteading in any city which adopts an ordinance to administer a program in accordance with state statutes.

HOMESTEAD

ALABAMA	
Value Limit	$6,000
Area Limit	160 acres
ALASKA	
Value Limit	$27,000
Area Limit	Must be prinicipal residence
ARIZONA	
Value Limit	$50,000
Area Limit	Must be residence
ARKANSAS	
Value Limit	$2,500
Area Limit	One acre in city, town or village; 160 acres elsewhere
CALIFORNIA	
Value Limit	$45,000 if spouse is 65 or older or member of family unit; 30,000 for others
Area Limit	Must be actual residence
COLORADO	
Value Limit	$20,000
Area Limit	None
FLORIDA	
Value Limit	None except only $1,000 of personal property
Area Limit	One-half acre in city or town; 160 acres elsewhere

GEORGIA

Value Limit	$500 (in town or city) $200 (elsewhere)
Area Limit	50 acres outside of town or city

HAWAII

Value Limit	$20,000 (head of family or over 65 years of age) $10,000 (others)
Area Limit	1 acre in "one piece of land"

IDAHO

Value Limit	$25,000 (head of family) $12,000 (others)
Area Limit	None

ILLINOIS

Value Limit	$7,500
Area Limit	None

IOWA

Value Limit	$500
Area Limit	One-half acre in city of town; 40 acres elsewhere

KANSAS

Value Limit	None
Area Limit	1 acre in city or town; 160 acres of farm land

KENTUCKY

Value Limit	$5,000
Area Limit	None

LOUISIANA

Value Limit	$15,000
Area Limit	160 acres

MAINE

Value Limit	$7,500
Area Limit	Must be residence or burial plot

MASSACHUSETTS

Value Limit	$60,000
Area Limit	None

MICHIGAN

Value Limit	$3,500
Area Limit	1 lot in city, town or village; 40 acres elsewhere

MINNESOTA

Value Limit	None
Area Limit	One-half acre in city, village or borough; 80 acres elsewhere

MISSISSIPPI

Value Limit	$30,000
Area Limit	160 acres

MISSOURI

Value Limit	$5,000
Area Limit	None

MONTANA

Value Limit	$40,000
Area Limit	One-quarter acre in city or town; one acre of non-agricultural land not in municipality; 320 acres of agricultural land

NEBRASKA

Value Limit	$6,500
Area Limit	2 lots in city of village; 160 acres in country

NEVADA

Value Limit	90,000
Area Limit	None

NEW HAMPSHIRE

Value Limit	$5,000
Area Limit	None

NEW MEXICO

Value Limit	$20,000
Area Limit	None

NEW YORK

Value Limit	$10,000
Area Limit	None

NORTH CAROLINA

Value Limit	$1,000
Area Limit	None

NORTH DAKOTA

Value Limit	$80,000
Area Limit	Must be residence

OHIO

Value Limit	$1,000
Area Limit	None

OKLAHOMA

Value Limit	$5,000
Area Limit	160 acres if rural; 1 acre if urban

OREGON

Value Limit	$15,000 (one debtor) $20,000 (two or more debtors)
Area Limit	1 block in city; 160 acres elsewhere

SOUTH CAROLINA

Value Limit	$1,000
Area Limit	None

SOUTH DAKOTA

Value Limit	$30,000
Area Limit	1 acre in town; 160 acres in country

TENNESSEE

Value Limit	$7,500 if principal residence; otherwise $5,000
Area Limit	None

TEXAS	
Value Limit	None
Area Limit	200 acres for family; 100 acres for single adult
UTAH	
Value Limit	$8,000 for head of family, $2,000 for spouse, $500 for dependent
Area Limit	None
VERMONT	
Value Limit	$30,000
Area Limit	None
VIRGINIA	
Value Limit	$5,000
Area Limit	None
WASHINGTON	
Value Limit	$25,000
Area Limit	None
WEST VIRGINIA	
Value Limit	$5,000
Area Limit	None
WISCONSIN	
Value Limit	$25,000
Area Limit	40 acres of agricultural land; one-quarter acre otherwise
WYOMING	
Value Limit	$10,000
Area Limit	None

FAMILY ALLOWANCES—By statute in most states, provision is made for the support and maintenance of the surviving spouse and children out of the estate of the decedent. The right is usually confined to the widow and children, although some statutes provide an allownace for the widow, widower or survivor. These allowances cannot be defeated by Will and become a charge on the estate whether or not it is solvent.

In many jurisdictions the widow is entitled to specified articles from the estate such as household furniture, clothing, etc. In some cases the specified property is in addition to allowance provided for support. The purpose of allowances for maintenance of the family is to provide support until the estate is distributed; it is usually limited in time from six months to one year. In some states the widow is not entitled to maintenance where she has separate property of a specified amount.

RIGHT OF ELECTION— **a. Dower or Curtesy and Intestate Share:** Under many statutes which allow dower or curtesy, the spouse is granted the right to elect between the share taken by dower or curtesy and a certain distributive or intestate share. The statutes provide which share shall be taken, if an election is not made; the time within which the election must be made varies from state to state. The election must generally be exercised by the surviving spouse during his or her lifetime.

b. Election Between Will and Distributive Share: Neither spouse may disinherit the other, in most states. Where one spouse dies leaving a Will which fails to provide for the survivor in any way, or provides a lesser amount than would have been taken had the testator died without a Will, the survivor may take the property under the Will or exercise a right of election. The right of election permits the survivor to elect to take that distributive share provided by law, as against that which would have been taken under the Will.

Most states allow either spouse the right to elect, although the shares taken may be different. In states where common law dower or curtesy or their statutory substitute has been retained, a testator cannot defeat by Will the share which the survivor would take. In some states the dissenting spouse takes a share in the personal property in addition to dower or curtesy while other states provide for intestate share to the survivor.

The prohibition against disinheritance by a testator is not absolute, even in states where the spouse has a right of election. The misconduct of the surviving spouse may effectively bar the right of election. In Connecticut, abandonment continuing to the time of the testator's death, without sufficient cause, results in a forfeiture of the statutory share of inheritance. Adultery, desertion or failure to support may also result in a forfeiture.

Statutes usually provide a fixed period of time during which the election must be made. The right to elect is a personal right, however, and must be exercised by the surviving spouse during his or her lifetime.

In community property states the survivor takes at least one-half of all community property, even though the testator attempts to will the survivor's share to another.

The following chart illustrates the Spouse's Right of Election, indicating the shares which may be taken as against the Will. Where an intestate share is allowed, the spouse inherits the same share that would have passed if there was no Will. Limitations on the share taken by election are included where they exist.

Dower or Curtesy as used here denotes the share a husband or wife could take, as provided in the table Dower, Curtesy and Statutory Substitutions and only indicates that the survivor takes the present statutory equivalent of Dower or Curtesy.

SPOUSE'S RIGHT OF ELECTION

ALABAMA

Election by Husband:	Yes
Election by Wife:	Yes
Limitation or Share:	Lesser of decedent's estate reduced by value of survivors estate or one-third of decedents estate
Period for Filing:	Within 6 months after decedent's death or after probate

ALASKA

Election by Husband:	Yes
Election by Wife:	Yes
Limitation or Share:	One-third of augmented net estate
Period for Filing:	Within 9 months after death or within 6 months after probate

ARKANSAS

Election by Husband:	Yes
Election by Wife:	Yes
Limitation or Share:	Intestate share
Period for Filing:	Within 1 month after expiration for filing claims

COLORADO

Election by Husband:	Yes
Election by Wife:	Yes
Limitation or Share:	One-half of augmented net estate
Period for Filing:	Within 6 months after notice for filing claims or 1 year after death

CONNECTICUT

Election by Husband:	Yes
Election by Wife:	Yes
Limitation or Share:	One-third of estate for life
Period for Filing:	Within two months after expiration for filing claims

DELAWARE

Election by Husband:	Yes
Election by Wife:	Yes
Limitation or Share:	$20,000 or one-third of estate, whichever is less
Period for Filing:	Within 6 months after grant of Letters Testamentary or of Administration

DISTRICT OF COLUMBIA

Election by Husband:	Yes
Election by Wife:	Yes
Limitation or Share:	Intestate share up to one-half of estate
Period for Filing:	Within 6 months after probate

FLORIDA

Election by Husband:	Yes
Election by Wife:	Yes
Limitation or Share:	30% of net assets
Period for Filing:	Within 4 months of notice of administration

HAWAII

Election by Husband:	Yes
Election by Wife:	Yes
Limitation or Share:	One-third of net estate
Period for Filing:	Within 9 months after death or 6 months after probate

IDAHO

Election by Husband:	Yes
Election by Wife:	Yes
Limitation or Share:	One-half of quasi community property
Period for Filing:	With 6 months after publication of first notice to creditors

ILLINOIS

Election by Husband:	Yes
Election by Wife:	Yes
Limitation or Share:	If descendants survive, one-third of entire estate; if not, one-half of entire estate
Period for Filing:	Within 7 months after probate

INDIANA

Election by Husband:	Yes
Election by Wife:	Yes
Limitation or Share:	One-third of entire estate. If surviving spouse is a second or subsequent spouse who did not have children by the decedent and the decedent left a child or decedent, then the share is limited to one-third of the net personal estate plus a life estate in one-third of the real property.
Period for Filing:	Within 10 days after time for filing claims

IOWA

Election by Husband:	Yes
Election by Wife:	Yes
Limitation or Share:	Intestate share
Period for Filing:	Within 4 months after second notice of probate

KANSAS

Election by Husband:	Yes
Election by Wife:	Yes
Limitation or Share:	Intestate share
Period for Filing:	Within 4 months after probate

KENTUCKY

Election by Husband:	Yes
Election by Wife:	Yes
Limitation or Share:	Dower or curtesy limited to one-third of real property
Period for Filing:	Within 6 months after probate

MAINE

Election by Husband:	Yes
Election by Wife:	Yes
Limitation or Share:	One-third of augmented net estate
Period for Filing:	Within 6 months after probate or 9 months after death

MARYLAND

Election by Husband:	Yes
Election by Wife:	Yes
Limitation or Share:	Intestate share
Period for Filing:	Within 30 days after time for filing claims has expired

MASSACHUSETTS

Election by Husband:	Yes
Election by Wife:	Yes
Limitation or Share:	One-third of estate if issues survive. If testator leaves no issue or kindred, surviving spouse takes $25,000 plus one-half of remainder. If testator leaves kindred but no issue, surviving spouse takes $25,000 plus income of one-half of personal property in trust and income from one-half of real property for life
Period for Filing:	Within 6 months after probate

MICHIGAN

Election by Husband:	Yes
Election by Wife:	Yes
Limitation or Share:	One-half of intestate share reduced by one-half of value of property derived from decedent otherwise then by Will or intestate succession
Period for Filing:	Within 60 days after date for presentation of claims or 60 days after service of inventory, whichever is later

MINNESOTA

Election by Husband:	Yes
Election by Wife:	Yes
Limitation or Share:	Intestate share limited to one-half of entire estate if no surviving issue
Period for Filing:	Within 6 months after probate, or 9 months after death

MISSISSIPPI

Election by Husband:	Yes
Election by Wife:	Yes
Limitation or Share:	Intestate share limited to one-half of entire estate. If surviving spouse has separate property amounting to more than a one-fifth share of the estate, the survivor can only elect to take the difference between the separate property and the share entitled to under the election.
Period for Filing:	Within 90 days after probate

MISSOURI

Election by Husband:	Yes
Election by Wife:	Yes
Limitation or Share:	One-third of estate if lineal descendants survive, otherwise one-half
Period for Filing:	10 days after time limited for contesting Will or within 90 days after final determination of litigation

MONTANA

Election by Husband:	Yes
Election by Wife:	Yes
Limitation or Share:	One third of augmented estate
Period for Filing:	Within 6 months after probate, or 9 months after death

NEBRASKA

Election by Husband:	Yes
Election by Wife:	Yes
Limitation or Share:	One-half of augmented estate
Period for Filing:	Within 6 months after publication of notice to creditors or within one year after death, whichever occurs first

NEW HAMPSHIRE

Election by Husband:	Yes
Election by Wife:	Yes
Limitation or Share:	Intestate share
Period for Filing:	Within 6 months after appointment of Executor

NEW JERSEY

Election by Husband:	Yes
Election by Wife:	Yes
Limitation or Share:	One-third of augmented estate
Period for Filing:	Within 6 months after probate

NEW YORK

Election by Husband:	Yes
Election by Wife:	Yes
Limitation or Share:	Intestate share limited to one-half of net estate; one-third if issue survive. In some instances certain absolute legacies or trust provisions may defeat the right of election. (See E.P.T.L. §5-1.1)
Period for Filing:	Within 6 months after issuance of letters testamentary or letters of administration with Will annexed

NORTH CAROLINA

Election by Husband:	Yes
Election by Wife:	Yes
Limitation or Share:	Intestate share, limited to one-half of the estate
Period for Filing:	Within 6 months after issuance of letters testamentary or of administration

NORTH DAKOTA

Election by Husband:	Yes
Election by Wife:	Yes
Limitation or Share:	One-third of augmented estate
Period for Filing:	Within 9 months after death or 6 months after probate

OHIO

Election by Husband:	Yes
Election by Wife:	Yes
Limitation or Share:	Intestate share limited to one-half of estate; if two or more children or lineal descendents survive then limited to one-third
Period for Filing:	Within 1 months after service of citation to elect

OKLAHOMA

Election by Husband:	Yes
Election by Wife:	Yes
Limitation or Share:	Intestate share
Period for Filing:	No fixed period

OREGON

Election by Husband:	Yes
Election by Wife:	Yes
Limitation or Share:	One-fourth of net estate. The net estate may be reduced by certain property given under the Will
Period for Filing:	Within 90 days after admission of Will to probate or 30 days after filing inventory

PENNSYLVANIA

Election by Husband:	Yes
Election by Wife:	Yes
Limitation or Share:	One-third of estate
Period for Filing:	Within 6 months after probate

RHODE ISLAND

Election by Husband:	Yes
Election by Wife:	Yes
Limitation or Share:	Life estate in real property
Period for Filing:	Within 6 months after probate

SOUTH CAROLINA

Election by Husband:	Yes
Election by Wife:	Yes
Limitation or Share:	Dower
Period for Filing:	Prior to distribution of estate, or when called to renounce her dower interest

TENNESSEE

Election by Husband:	Yes
Election by Wife:	Yes
Limitation or Share:	One-third of net estate
Period for Filing:	Within 6 months after probate or within 9 months after death

UTAH

Election by Husband:	Yes
Election by Wife:	Yes
Limitation or Share:	One-third of augmented estate
Period for Filing:	Within one year after death or within 6 months after probate

VERMONT

Election by Husband:	Yes
Election by Wife:	Yes
Limitation or Share:	Dower or curtesy
Period for Filing:	Within 8 months after probate

VIRGINIA

Election by Husband:	Yes
Election by Wife:	Yes
Limitation or Share:	Dower or curtesy plus one-third of personal property if issue or adopted child survive, otherwise one-half
Period for Filing:	Within one year after probate

WEST VIRGINIA

Election by Husband:	Yes
Election by Wife:	Yes
Limitation or Share:	Intestate share
Period for Filing:	Within 8 months of probate

WISCONSIN

Election by Husband:	Yes
Election by Wife:	Yes
Limitation or Share:	One-third of net estate
Period for Filing:	Within 6 months after death

WYOMING

Election by Husband:	Yes
Election by Wife:	Yes
Limitation or Share:	Intestate share of entire estate, limited to one-fourth if children survive; one-half if no children survive
Period for Filing:	Within 3 months after probate

EFFECT OF DIVORCE, SEPARATION AND ANNULMENT. a. **Divorce:** A decree of absolute divorce terminates the marital relationship and deprives each spouse of any right to inherit any property from the other under the laws of intestacy. The divorce decree must be final. An interlocutory decree which requires that a period of time must elapse before the decree is final does not affect the inheritance rights of either spouse.

b. **Separation:** Where a husband and wife are living apart at the time that one of them dies, the survivor is not precluded from inheriting from the deceased spouse. This rule does not necessarily apply where one spouse abandons the other without just cause. The separation of husband and wife, whether or not judicially decreed, does not dissolve the marriage. A husband and wife may enter into a separation agreement, in most jurisdictions, and release to each other any rights of inheritance which may accrue. Where such a valid contract is entered into, the surviving spouse will be barred from inheriting from the estate of the decedent. A separation agreement which is subsequently abrogated by a reconciliation of husband and wife, does not prevent either spouse from sharing in the estate of the other.

c. **Annulment:** An annulment is a judicial declaration that a voidable marriage no longer exists; therefore neither party has any rights of inheritance in the estate of the other. If the marriage is voidable but no annulment was obtained, the parties will inherit from each other as husband and wife.

If a marriage is void, the relationship of husband and wife never existed, and no right to share in each other's estate as husband and wife would exist.

SUMMARY OF STATE LAWS

ALABAMA The surviving spouse inherits the entire estate if there is no surviving issue or parent of the decedent. If the decedent is survived by a parent but no surviving issue the surviving spouse inherits $100,000 plus one-half of the balance. If the decedent is survived by issue all of whom are issue of the surviving spouse also, the surviving spouse inherits $50,000 plus one-half of the balance. If there are surviving issue one or more of whom are not the issue of the surviving spouse, then the surviving spouse inherits one-half of the intestate estate (§2-102).

ALASKA The surviving spouse inherits the entire estate if there is no surviving child or parent of the decedent. If the decedent is survived by a parent or a child who is also the child of the surviving spouse, the spouse inherits the first $50,000 plus one-half of the balance of the estate. The surviving spouse inherits one-half of the estate if the decedent is survived by a child not the issue of his surviving spouse (§13.11.010).

ARIZONA **Community Property:** Upon the death of the husband or wife one-half of the community property passes to the survivor. If the decedent is not survived by descendants, the spouse inherits all the community property (§14-2102).

Separate Property: The surviving spouse inherits the entire intestate estate if the decedent is not survived by a child, or if survived by a child who is also the issue of the surviving spouse. If the decedent is survived by a child who is not the issue of the surviving spouse, then the spouse inherits one-half of the separate property (§14-2102).

ARKANSAS In addition to dower and curtesy, the surviving spouse inherits one-third of the personal estate(§61-202). If the decedent is not survived by a descendant, the surviving spouse inherits the entire estate. However, if the decedent and the surviving spouse had been continually married less than three years, the surviving spouse inherits fifty percent of the estate (§61-149).

CALIFORNIA **Community Property:** Upon the death of husband or wife, one-half of the community property goes to the survivor. If the other half is not disposed of by Will, it goes to the survivor (Prob. C. §201).

Separate Property: The surviving spouse inherits as follows—One-half of the entire estate if the decedent leaves one child or the issue of a deceased child; one-third, if the decedent leaves more than one child, or one child and the issue of one or more deceased children (Prob. C §221). The spouse takes one-half, if the decedent leaves no issue but is survived by either parent, brothers or sisters or their descendants (Prob. C §223). The spouse inherits the entire estate if neither issue, parent, brother, sister, nor descendant of deceased brother or sister, survive the decedent (Prob. C. §224).

COLORADO The surviving spouse inherits the entire estate if there is no surviving issue of the decedent. If the decedent is survived by issue who is also issue of the surviving spouse, then the spouse takes the first $25,000 plus one-half of the balance of the estate. The surviving spouse inherits one-half of the estate if the decedent is survived by issue not the issue of the surviving spouse (§15-11-102).

CONNECTICUT If the decedent is survived by issue who is also the issue of the surviving spouse, then the spouse takes the first $50,000 plus one-half of the balance of the estate. The surviving spouse inherits one-half of the estate if the decedent is survived by issue not the issue of the surviving spouse. If the decedent is survived by a parent but no children or their representatives, the spouse inherits $50,000 plus three-quarters of the remainder. The spouse inherits the entire estate if the decedent is survived by no children or representatives of children and no parent (§45-273a).

DELAWARE The surviving spouse inherits the entire estate if the decedent leaves no surviving issue or parent. If the decedent is survived by a parent or by issue also the issue of the surviving spouse, then the spouse inherits the first $50,000 plus one-half of the intestate personal estate and a life estate in the intestate real estate. If the decedent is survived by issue one or more of whom are not the issue of the surviving spouse, then the spouse inherits one-half of the intestate personal estate and a life estate in the intestate real estate (T. 12 §502).

DISTRICT OF COLUMBIA **Real Property:** In addition to the right of dower, the surviving spouse inherits real property in the same proportion as personal property (§19-301).

Personal Property: The surviving spouse inherits one-third of all personal property if decedent is survived by a child or descendants (§19-303). If the decedent is survived by no child or descendants but by either parent, and brother, sister or children of deceased brothers and sisters, the spouse inherits one-half (§19-304). If the decedent is survived by none of the above mentioned, the spouse inherits all personal property (§19-302).

FLORIDA The surviving spouse inherits the entire estate if there is no surviving lineal descendant of the decedent. If there are surviving lineal descendants all of whom are lineal descendants of the surviving spouse also, then the spouse takes the first $20,000 plus one-half of the balance of the estate. The surviving spouse takes one-half of the estate if the decedent is survived by lineal descendants one or more of whom are not lineal descendants of the surviving spouse (§732.102).

GEORGIA The surviving spouse inherits a child's share of the entire estate if the decedent is survived by children or their descendants; however, if there are more than five shares, the widow is entitled to one-fifth. The surviving spouse inherits the entire estate if the decedent leaves no children or descendants (§§53-4-2,3).

HAWAII If there is no surviving issue or parent of the decedent, the surviving spouse inherits the entire estate. If there is surviving issue or parent of the decedent, the surviving spouse inherits one-half of the estate. (§560:2-202)

IDAHO **Community Property:** The one-half of community property which belongs to the decedent passes to the surviving spouse if not disposed of by Will (§15-2-102).

Separate Property: The surviving spouse inherits the entire intestate estate if there is no surviving issue or parent of the decedent. If the decedent is survived by a parent or issue all of whom are issue of the surviving spouse, then the spouse takes the first $50,000 plus one-half of the balance of the estate. If the decedent is survived by issue one or more of whom are not the issue of the surviving spouse, then the spouse takes one-half of the estate (§15-2-102).

ILLINOIS The surviving spouse takes one-half of the estate if the decedent is survived by descendants. If no descendants survive the decedent, the surviving spouse takes the entire estate (Ch. 110½ §2-1).

INDIANA **Real Property:** The surviving spouse inherits one-third of the real property if the decedent is survived by two or more children or their descendants. If the decedent is survived by one child or the descendant of a deceased child, the surviving spouse takes one-half. The surviving spouse inherits three-fourths of the real property if the decedent leaves a parent surviving. If there are no surviving children, or descendants, or a parent, the surviving spouse inherits all the real property. If, however, the surviving spouse is a second or subsequent spouse who did not have any children, and the decedent left a child or descendants of a previous spouse, then the surviving spouse only takes a life estate in one-third of the real property.

Personal Property: The surviving spouse takes the same share of personal property as real property, except that it is not subject to the limitation outlined above, if the decedent was survived by issue not of the surviving spouse (29-1-2-1).

IOWA If the decedent left issue, the surviving spouse inherits one-third of the real property, all personal property in the hands of the decedent as head of the family exempt from execution and one-third of all other personal property; if this inheritance is valued at less than $50,000 the spouse is entitled to so much of the remaining estate as will make that amount (§633.211). If the decedent left no issue, the surviving spouse inherits (1) one-half of the real property; (2) all personal property in the hands of the decedent as head of the family, exempt from execution, and (3) one-half of all other personal property; if the value of (1) and (3) is less than $50,000 then the spouse is entitled to such additional real and personal property as will make that amount. The spouse also takes such additional property as necessary to make a total (including the aforementioned) inheritance of $50,000 plus one-half of the net value of the estate and all exempt personal property (§633.212).

KANSAS The surviving spouse inherits one-half of the entire estate if the decedent is survived by a child or children or issue of a previously deceased child or children. The surviving spouse inherits the entire estate if the decedent was not survived by a child or children or issue of a previously deceased child (§59-504).

KENTUCKY In addition to dower or curtesy, the surviving spouse inherits one-half of all personal property (§391.030). The survivor inherits the entire estate if the decedent is not survived by either children or descendants, parent, brothers or sisters or their descendants (§390.010).

LOUISIANA **Community Property:** If the deceased leaves no descendants, the surviving spouse inherits the community property (Civil Code Art. 889). If the deceased spouse is survived by descendants and has not disposed of the descendant's share of community property by Will, then the surviving spouse takes a legal usufruct (i.e. the use of real property) over so much of that share as may be inherited by the descendants. This usufruct terminates when the surviving spouse remarries. (Civil Code Art. 890).

Separate Property: If the deceased leaves neither descendants nor parents, nor brothers, sisters, or descendants from them, the surviving spouse not judicially separated from the deceased inherits the separate property to the exclusion of other ascendants and collaterals (Civil Code Art. 894).

MAINE The surviving spouse inherits the entire estate if there is no surviving issue or parent of the decendent. If the decedent is survived by a parent but no surviving issue, the surviving spouse inherits $50,000 plus one-half of the balance. If the decedent is survived by issue all of whom are issue of the surviving spouse also, the surviving spouse inherits $50,000 plus one-half of the balance. If there are surviving issue, one or more of whom are not the issue of the surviving spouse, then the surviving spouse inherits one-half of the intestate estate (T.18A §2-102).

MARYLAND The surviving spouse inherits one-half of the estate if there is a surviving minor child. If there is no surviving minor child but there is surviving issue then the surviving spouse inherits the first $15,000 plus one-half of the residue. If there is no surviving issue but a surviving parent the surviving spouse inherits the first $15,000 plus one-half of the residue. The surviving spouse inherits the entire estate if there is no surviving issue or parent (§3-102).

MASSACHUSETTS The surviving spouse inherits an

intestate share of the estate, unless an election to take dower or curtesy is made within six months after the approval of the administrator's or executor's bond (ch.189 §1). The survivor's intestate share is as follows: One-half of the estate if the decedent is survived by issue; $50,000 and one-half of the excess if kindred but no issue survive the decedent. If no kindred survive, the survivor inherits the entire estate (ch.190 §1).

MICHIGAN If a decedent domiciled in the state dies intestate, the surviving widow shall elect between her intestate share and her dower right (§700.282a). The intestate share of the surviving spouse is as follows: If there is not a surviving issue or parent of the decedent, the entire estate; if there is not a surviving issue but the decedent is survived by at least one parent the first $60,000 which shall be reduced in case of partial intestacy by any amount given the spouse by will, plus one-half of the balance of the estate; if there are surviving issue all of whom are issue of the surviving spouse also, the first $60,000 plus one-half of the balance of the estate; if there are surviving issue, one or more of whom are not the issue of the surviving spouse, one-half of the intestate estate (§700.105).

MINNESOTA The surviving spouse inherits one-third of the estate of more than one child or one child and issue of a deceased child or issue of two or more deceased children survive the decedent. If the decedent is survived by one child or the issue of one deceased child, the surviving spouse inherits one-half of the estate. If no issue or descendants survive the decedent, the survivor inherits the entire estate (§525.16). The surviving spouse takes the above-mentioned proportionate interest in all real property of which the decedent, while married to such spouse, was seized or possessed, to the disposition whereof such survivor shall not have consented in writing (§525.16).

MISSISSIPPI If children or their descendants survive the decedent, the surviving spouse inherits a child's share. If no children, or descendants survive the decedent, the survivor inherits the entire estate (§91-1-7).

MISSOURI The surviving spouse inherits the entire estate if there is no surviving issue or parent of the decedent. If the decedent is survived by a parent but no surviving issue, the surviving spouse inherits $20,000 plus one-half of the balance. If the decedent is survived by issue all of whom are issue of the surviving spouse also, the surviving spouse inherits $20,000 plus one-half of the balance. If there are surviving issue one or more of whom are not the issue of the surviving spouse, then the surviving spouse inherits one-half of the intestate estate (§474.10).

MONTANA The surviving spouse inherits the entire estate if the decedent leaves no issue or if there are surviving issue all of whom are the issue of the surviving spouse. If the decedent is survived by one child not the issue of the surviving spouse, or the issue of one such child, then the surviving spouse takes one-half of the estate. If the decedent is survived by more than one child all of whom are not the issue of the surviving spouse or one such child and the issue of one or more such children, the surviving spouse takes one-third of the estate (§72-2-202).

NEBRASKA The surviving spouse inherits the entire estate if there is no surviving issue or parent of the decedent. If the decedent is survived by a parent but no surviving issue, the surviving spouse inherits $50,000 plus one-half of the balance. If the decedent is survived by issue all of whom are issue of the surviving spouse also, the surviving spouse inherits $50,000 plus one-half of the balance. If there are surviving issue one or more of whom are not the issue of the surviving spouse, then the surviving spouse inherits one-half of the intestate estate (§30-2302).

NEVADA Community Property: The surviving spouse takes all the community property subject to the testamenatry disposition of one-half by the decedent (§123-250).

Separate Property: The surviving spouse inherits the following share, subject to the decedent's debts: One-third if more than one child, or one child and descendants of one deceased child, or descendants of two or more deceased children survive the decedent. The survivor inherits one-half, if one child, descendants of deceased child, parent, brother, sister or issue of a deceased brother or sister survive the decedent. If none of the last mentioned relatives survive, the spouse inherits all separate property (§134.030-.050).

NEW HAMPSHIRE The surviving spouse inherits the entire estate if the decedent is not survived by issue or a parent. If there is no surviving issue but the decedent is survived by a parent or parents, the surviving spouse takes $50,000 plus one-half of the balance of the estate. If the decedent leaves issue all of whom are the issue of the surviving spouse, then the spouse takes $50,000 plus one-half of the balance of the estate. If there are surviving issue one or more of whom are not the issue of the surviving spouse, then the spouse inherits one-half of the estate (§561:1).

Intestate share under election against will: If the surviving spouse elects to waive all homestead rights and the provisions of the decedent's will, the following share is taken: If the decedent leaves no issue, one-third of the estate; if the decedent leaves no issue but is survived by a parent, brother or sister, the spouse takes $10,000 in personal property and $10,000 in value of real property plus one-half of the remainder; the real estate to be assigned in the same manner as dower; if the decedent leaves no parent, brother or sister, the spouse takes $10,000 plus $2,000 for each full year from the date of marriage to the decedent plus one-half of the remainder; the real estate to be assigned in the same manner as dower (§560:10).

NEW JERSEY The surviving spouse inherits the entire estate if there is no surviving issue or parent of the decedent. If the decedent is survived by a parent but no surviving issue, the surviving spouse inherits $50,000 plus one-half of the balance. If the decedent is survived by issue all of whom are issue of the surviving spouse also, the surviving spouse inherits $50,000 plus one-half of the balance. If there are surviving issue one or more of whom are not the issue of the surviving spouse, then the surviving spouse inherits one-half of the intestate estate. (T.3B:5 §3)

NEW MEXICO **Community Property:** The surviving spouse takes all the community property subject to the disposition of one-half by the decedent (§45-2-804).

Separate Property: The surviving spouse inherits one-fourth of all separate property if issue survive the decedent. If no issue survive, the survivor inherits the whole estate (§45-2-102).

NEW YORK The surviving spouse inherits money or personal property not exceeding $4,000 plus one-third of the entire estate if children or descendants survive the decedent.

In a case where one child survives but no issue of a deceased child, or where there are no surviving children but issue of a deceased child, then the surviving spouse inherits money or personal property not exceeding $4,000 plus one-half of the estate.

If the decedent is survived by a parent but no issue, the survivor takes $25,000 and one-half of the excess. The surviving spouse inherits the entire estate if the decedent is survived by neither children, descendants or parent (E.P.T.L. §4-1.1).

NORTH CAROLINA **Real Property:** If the intestate is survived by only one child or by any lineal descendant of only one child, the surviving spouse inherits a one-half undivided interest in real property. If the intestate is survived by two or more children or by one child and any lineal descendent of one or more deceased children or by lineal descendants of two or more deceased children, the surviving spouse inherits a one-third undivided interest in real property. If the intestate is not survived by a child or a lineal descendant but is survived by a parent, the surviving spouse inherits a one-half undivided interest in real property. If the intestate is not survived by a child, a lineal descendant or parent, the surviving spouse inherits all the real property.

Personal Property: If the intestate is not survived by a child, or any lineal descendant or a parent, the surviving spouse inherits all the personal property. If the intestate is survived by only one child or by a lineal descendant of only one child, and the net personal property does not exceed $15,000 the surviving spouse inherits all; if the net personal property exceeds $15,000 then the surviving spouse inherits $15,000 plus one-half of the balance. If the intestate is survived by two or more children or by one child and only lineal descendant of one or more deceased children or by lineal descendants of two or more deceased children and the net personal property does not exceed $15,000 the surviving spouse inherits all; if the net personal property exceeds $15,000 then the surviving spouse inherits $15,000 plus one-third of the balance. If the intestate is not survived by a child or lineal descendant but is survived by a parent and the net personal property does not exceed $25,000 the surviving spouse inherits all; if the property exceeds $25,000 then the surviving spouse inherits $25,000 plus one-half of the balance. (§29-14).

NORTH DAKOTA The surviving spouse inherits the entire estate if the decedent leaves no surviving issue or parent. If there is no surviving issue but the decedent is survived by a parent, the surviving spouse inherits the first $50,000 plus one-half of the balance of the estate. If there are surviving issue all of whom are issue of the surviving spouse also, the spouse inherits the first $50,000 plus one-half of the balance of the estate. If there are surviving issue one or more of whom are not issue of the surviving spouse, the spouse takes one-half of the estate (§30.1-04-02).

OHIO The surviving husband or wife takes dower only in those lands which were conveyed or incumbered during the lifetime of both, without the consent of the other spouse. There is no vested dower in lands owned by the decedent at his death. In lieu of such dower interest as terminates and is barred, pursuant to the statutes, the surviving spouse is entitled to the intestate share provided by the laws of inheritance (§2103.02).

If the decedent is survived by one child or his lineal descendant, the surviving spouse inherits the first $30,000 if the spouse is the natural or adoptive parent or the first $10,000 if the spouse is not the natural or adoptive parent, plus one-half of the balance of the estate. If the decedent is survived by more than one child or their lineal descendants the spouse inherits the first $30,000 if the spouse is the natural or adoptive parent or the first $10,000 if the spouse is not the natural or adoptive parent plus one-third of the balance. The surviving spouse inherits the entire estate if the decedent is not survived by children or lineal descendants (§2105.06).

OKLAHOMA The surviving spouse inherits one-half of the entire estate if the decedent is survived by one child or the issue of one deceased child. If the decedent is survived by more than one child or one child and the issue of the deceased child or issue of two or more deceased children, the spouse takes one-third. However, if the decedent was married more than once, the spouse at death takes only a child's share with living children and issue of deceased children in that property which was not acquired during the marriage. If no issue but a parent, brother or sister survive the decedent, the surviving spouse inherits one-half. However, the survivor inherits all property which was acquired during the marriage by the joint industry of husband and wife, if the decedent is not survived by issue. The surviving spouse takes the entire estate if neither issue, parent, brother or sister survive the decedent (T.84 §213).

OREGON The surviving spouse inherits one-half of the estate if the decedent is survived by issue (§112.025). If no issue survive, the surviving spouse inherits the entire estate (§112.035).

PENNSYLVANIA The surviving spouse inherits the entire estate if there is no surviving issue or parent of the decedent. If the decedent is survived by a parent but no surviving issue, the surviving spouse inherits $30,000 plus one-half of the balance. If the decedent is survived by issue all of whom are issue of the surviving spouse also, the surviving spouse inherits $30,000 plus one-half of the balance. If there are surviving issue one or more of whom are not the issue of the surviving spouse, then the surviving spouse inherits one-half of the intestate estate (T.20 §2102).

RHODE ISLAND In addition to dower or curtesy in real property, the surviving spouse takes one-half of the personal property if the decedent is survived by issue (§33-1-10). If no issue survive the decedent, the survivor takes $50,000 and one-half of personal property and a life estate in all real estate property (§§33-1-5, 10). If the decedent is survived by neither maternal nor paternal kindred, the surviving spouse takes the entire estate (§33-1-3).

SOUTH CARONLINA The widow takes dower, unless she accepts her distributive share of the estate which, if accepted, is in lieu of and is in bar of dower. If the widow forfeits her dower, she shall also forfeit her intestate share of her husband's real property (§21-3-70).

Subject to the exceptions above, the surviving spouse inherits the following share of all real and personal property; One-half if the decedent is survived by one child or descendants of a deceased child; one-third if the decedent is survived by more than one child or their descendants. The surviving spouse inherits one-half of the estate if the decedent is survived by no children or issue but was survived by a parent or other ancestor, brother, sister, of either whole or half-blood or nephew or niece of the whole-blood. The survivor inherits the entire estate if none of the above mentioned survive the decedent (§21-3-20).

SOUTH DAKOTA If the decedent leaves a surviving spouse and more than one child or one child and the issue of a deceased child or the issue of two or more deceased children, the survivor inherits one-third of the estate (§29-1-5). If one child or the issue of a deceased child survive the decedent, the surviving spouse inherits one-half of the estate (§29-1-5). The spouse inherits $100,000 and one-half of the excess, if decedent is survived by no issue but a parent, brother or sister or descendants of deceased brothers and sisters (§29-1-6). If the decedent leaves a surviving husband or wife and no issue, and no parent or brother, nor sister, the whole estate shall go to the surviving husband or wife (§29-1-8).

TENNESSEE If there is no surviving issue of the decedent, the surviving spouse inherits the entire intestate estate. If there are surviving issue of the decedent, the surviving spouse inherits one-third or a childs share of the entire intestate estate, whichever is greater (§31-203). "Issue" of a person is defined to mean all his lineal descendants (adopted as well as natural born) of all generations, with the relationship of parent and child at each generation (§31-101).

TEXAS **Community Property:** On the death of either husband or wife, all community property passes to the survivor, if the decedent is survived by neither children or descendants. If the decedent is survived by any children or descendants, the surviving spouse takes one half of the community property (Prob. C. §38).

Separate Property: If the deceased leaves a child, children, or descendants, the surviving husband or wife takes one-third of the personal estate and a life estate in one-third of the real property. If no children or descendants survive the decedent, the spouse inherits all the personal property and one-half of all real property absolutely. If the deceased has neither issue, parent, brothers, sisters nor their descendants surviving, the entire estate passes to the surviving spouse (Prob. C. §38).

UTAH The surviving spouse inherits the entire estate if there is no surviving issue or parent of the decedent. If the decedent is survived by a parent but no surviving issue, the surviving spouse inherits $100,000 plus one-half of the balance. If the decedent is survived by issue all of whom are issue of the surviving spouse also, the surviving spouse inherits $50,000 plus one-half of the balance. If there are surviving issue one or more of whom are not the issue of the surviving spouse, then the surviving spouse inherits one-half of the intestate estate (§375-2-102).

VERMONT The surviving spouse takes dower or curtesy. Where the decedent is not survived by issue, the survivor takes an intestate share unless an election to take dower or curtesy is made within eight months after letters of administration are issued (T. 14 §465). The survivor inherits the whole estate up to $25,000 and one-half of the excess, if no issue survive. If the decedent has no kindred surviving, the spouse is entitled to the entire estate (T. 14 §551).

VIRGINIA **Real Property:** The surviving spouse takes a dower or curtest interest. In addition, the surviving spouse inherits the remaining real property interest unless the intestate is survived by children or their descendants, one or more of whom are not children or their descendants of the surviving spouse (§64.1-1).

Personal Property: If the decedent is survived by a child or descendants, the surviving spouse inherits one-third of the personal property. If no children or descendants survive, the surviving spouse is entitled to all personal property of the estate (§64.1-11).

WASHINGTON Community Property: Upon the death of either husband or wife, one-half of the community property shall go to the survivor. If no testamentary disposition is made of the remainder, and no issue or parents survive the decedent, the remainder of the community property passes to the surviving spouse.

Separate Property: The surviving spouse inherits one-half of the estate if the decedent is survived by issue. If the decedent leaves no issue but is survived by one or more parents or by the issue of one or more of his parents, the spouse takes three-quarters of the estate. The surviving spouse inherits the entire estate if the decedent leaves no issue nor parent nor issue of parent (§11.04.015).

WEST VIRGINIA **Real Property:** In addition to dower or curtesy, the surviving spouse takes all of the real property if the decedent is not survived by issue (c. 42 art. 1 §1).

Personal Property: If the decedent is survived by issue, the survivor inherits one-third; if no issue survive, the surviving spouse inherits all personal property (c. 42 art. 2 §1).

WISCONSIN The surviving spouse inherits the entire estate if the decedent leaves no surviving issue. If the decedent is survived by issue all of whom are the issue of the surviving spouse, the spouse takes the first $25,000 plus one-half of the balance where there is only one surviving child and no surviving issue of a deceased child or only the issue of one deceased child, but one-third of the balance in other cases. The surviving spouse inherits one-half of the estate if the decedent is survived by one child or the issue of a deceased child not the issue of the surviving spouse. In all other cases where the decedent left issue not the issue of the surviving spouse, the spouse inherits one-third of the estate (§852.01).

WYOMING The surviving spouse inherits one-half of the entire estate, if the decedent is survived by children or descendants. If no descendants but a parent, brother or sister survive the decedent, the spouse takes the whole estate up to $20,000 and three-fourths of the excess. If there be none of the aforementioned relatives of the intestate, the surviving spouse inherits the entire estate (§2-4-101).

Chapter 4

RIGHTS OF CHILDREN AND DESCENDANTS

IN GENERAL—A child's right of inheritance from parents is based on a "natural right" arising out of the close family relationship. At common law, the rules of inheritance favored the male child over the female as well as the right of the first born son over other children. Today, by statute in all states, the modern view is to recognize equal rights of children to inherit their parents' estate. Some jurisdictions still distinguish between real and personal property; however, the prevailing view is that all children inherit their parents' estate equally.

The inheritance rights of children in the parents' estate are subject, however, to the rights of the surviving spouse. In determining the share children take in the estate, it is always necessary to take into account dower, curtesy, homestead and other rights of the surviving spouse. Subject to the rights of the surviving spouse and the payment of debts, the children share in the estate equally. If one child survived the decedent, he would inherit the entire share; if four children survived, each child would take a one-fourth share.

DESCENDANTS OF A PREDECEASED CHILD—In determining the share each child takes, the law divides the estate into as many shares as there are surviving children and predeceased children, represented by issue. If parent A dies leaving children X and Y and grandchildren who were children of a predeceased son Z, each child would take one-third and the grandchildren would represent their parent Z. The grandchildren, being children of a predeceased child, are entitled to share in the estate to the same extent their parent would have shared if alive. If there were two grandchildren they would take one-third between them or one-sixth each. The issue represent their parent and share "per stirpes," which means they are entitled to share in the estate of an ancestor, in place of their parent.

Where children survive their parent, grandchildren do not as a group share in the grandparent's estate. The only time that grandchildren will inherit is when their parent, who was a child of the grandparent, was entitled to share in the estate.

Where descendants all stand in equal degree to the decedent, they share equally or "per capita." Therefore, if the decedent was survived by no children but by grandchildren, each grandchild would take an equal share. In that case they inherit equally in their own right, and not by representing their predeceased parent.

Where all children predecease their parent but leave issue who are of a different degree, the per stirpes rule would apply. If the decedent was survived by grandchildren and one grandchild who predeceased the grandparent leaving issue, the great-grandchildren would only share in the estate to the same extent as the previously deceased grandchild would have shared.

It is important in determining the inheritance rights of descendants, to keep two general rules in mind; 1. where the descendants are in equal degree to the ancestor they each take a like share, i.e., distribution per capita; 2. where the descendants are of unequal or different degree to the ancestor the representatives take and divide among themselves the same share their ancestor would have taken if alive, i.e., distribution per stirpes.

The majority of states provide for representation by descendants per stirpes where a child predeceased the parent; and per capita where all descendants are in equal degree to each other.

Under the Uniform Probate Code the first and principal division of the estate is to the generation which includes one or more living members (U.P.C. §2-106).

ADOPTED CHILDREN

a. **In General**—The common law did not recognize any rights of inheritance in other than blood relationships. All of our states have general statutory enactments regarding the relationship between foster child and foster parent; however, the inheritance rights arising out of this relationship are not, in the usual case, clearly defined.

b. **Inheritance From Foster Parents and Relatives**— The majority of our states specifically provide for inheritance by the child from the foster parents, while other states may be regarded as having the same rule by implication. A foster child does not usually inherit from the relatives of the adopting parents. This is the general rule of authority, although not usually set forth specifically by statute. An adoption creates a personal relationship between the adopted child and parents based on contract; therefore, it does not affect those who are not parties to the adoption.

c. **Inheritance from Natural Parents and Relatives**— Most states have no legislative provision concerning the right to inherit from natural parents and relatives, and the courts have generally held that the right to inherit remains. Some states allow the adopted child to inherit from natural parents by statutes. In California and Connecticut the child may not inherit from natural parents, while in Pennsylvania, although the right to inherit from natural parents is denied, inheritance from natural kin is allowed.

d. **Inheritance from Adopted Children**—The surviving spouse and descendants of an adopted child may, of course, inherit from him; but if he dies without leaving a spouse or descendants, the question arises as to which parents inherit. Generally, the adopting parents inherit from the adopted child.

The right of natural parents to inherit is not expressly conferred by any state and is specifically denied in some states. Natural relatives may not inherit, as a general rule. Where the state allows, the adopting parents and/or relatives the right to inherit, there is no need to deny expressly the right to the natural parents and relatives; obviously both cannot inherit the same property.

A distinction has been made in some states as to the source of property of the adopted child. Where the child receives his property from the natural family, the property should return to the natural family; and that which came from the adoptive family should return to the adoptive family.

Under the Uniform Probate Code, "an adopted child is the child of an adopting parent and not of the natural parents, except that adoption of a child by the spouse of a natural parent has no effect on the relationship between the child and that natural parent" (U.P.C. §2-109).

Due to the difference in statutory interpretation, it is extremely difficult to arrive at conclusions without considering specific fact situations and judicial interpretations.

ILLEGITIMATE CHILDREN—At early common law, the illegitimate child had no right of inheritance. The child was considered nullius filius and therefore incapable of inheriting or transmitting any estate. The rule was considered harsh and unjust, as it punished the offspring for the wrong of the parents, and has gradually changed through the years.

The inheritance rights of illegitimate children are usually limited. The general rule is that the illegitimate may inherit from his mother. In many states the child inherits from the mother in the same manner as if born in lawful wedlock, and in others, the illegitimate represents the mother as to inheritance from the mother's kindred. In states where the illegitimate inherits in the same manner as if legitimate, the states differ as to whether he inherits through the mother to the same extent as legitimate children.

In all states the mother inherits from her illegitimate offspring. Again, some statutes provide that she shall inherit in the same manner as if the child were legitimate, and therefore the right of the mother's kindred to inherit through the mother would exist. In many states the statutes provide specifically that the right to inherit would pass to the mother's kindred.

If the father of an illegitimate child acknowledges the child as his offspring, the child will usually inherit and transmit property as if he were legitimate. Some states require that the acknowledgement by the father be in writing, while other states require that the parents marry in addition to an acknowledgment by the father. The rules for legitimation are governed by the law of the father's domicile or permanent home.

Under the Uniform Probate Code, a person born out of wedlock is a child of the mother. That child is also a child of the father if the natural parents married before or after the birth of the child or the paternity is established by an adjudication. However, such adjudication is ineffective to qualify the father or his kindred to inherit from or through the child unless the father has openly treated the child as his, and has not refused to support the child (U.P.C. §2-109).

ADVANCEMENTS—If a child receives valuable property from an intestate parent during the latter's lifetime, it may be considered an advancement of the child's inheritance as the parent's heir. The ordinary expenses incurred by a parent for support, clothing and education, are not considered advancements. A nominal gift will not usually be considered an advancement.

All states have statutes concerning advancements. The majority of states consider an advancement as part of intestate parent's estate and deduct the value of the advancement from the share of the child advanced. If the child's share of the estate is more than the advancement, he receives the difference between the inheritance share and the advancement. If the advancement is greater than his share of the estate, the child takes nothing, although he need not refund the excess.

In some states, the child must put his advancement into the hotchpot or common fund of the estate in order to receive any inheritance from the parent's estate.

Some states require that the gift be expressed as an advancement and acknowledged in writing by the parent or the child. In New Hampshire a written acknowledgment is necessary, unless the gift is delivered expressly as an advancement in the presence of two witnesses.

In many states the advancement statutes apply not only to children but also to their issue. An advancement may, therefore, be charged against the inheritance of issue who represent a deceased child, although the representatives did not actually receive the advancement.

Under the Uniform Probate Code, the decedent's property which was given during his lifetime will be treated as an advancement only if declared in a contemporaneous writing by the decedent or acknowledged in writing by the heir (U.P.C. §2-110).

POSTHUMOUS CHILDREN—Children conceived but not born before the death of the father are entitled to inherit from the intestate father in the same manner as if born during his lifetime and had they survived him. The interest which the child takes at birth cannot be defeated by legal proceedings to which he was not a party.

BIRTH OF CHILDREN AFTER THE EXECUTION OF A WILL—Where states permit parents to disinherit their children, most of them require that the Will make some mention of them, to show an intention to disinherit at the time the Will was executed. The general rule is that a child born after the execution of a Will, and not provided for in the Will, may take part of the estate in spite of the Will. The birth of a child does not specifically revoke the Will but merely nullifies it in so far as it applies to the inheritance or part of the estate to which the child would have been entitled if there had been no Will. The fact that a child was born before the Will was executed, and no provision was made for him, does not in most jurisdictions have any effect; the after-born child may still claim his inheritance.

Chapter 5

RIGHTS OF SURVIVING PARENTS

IN GENERAL—Under the laws of inheritance parents are entitled to inherit, at least to some extent, the property of a deceased child leaving no descendants. The parents may be excluded from inheriting all or part of the estate if the decedent died leaving a spouse. Parents inherit to the exclusion of the decedent's brothers and sisters in most states, while some states allow the brothers and sisters to share in the estate with the decedent's parents.

At common law, parents did not inherit real property from an intestate child, even though the child left no heirs. This rule has since been abrogated by statute in all states. However, the parents' inheritance is always subject to existing rights of the surviving spouse. Also, the parents' right to inherit may be defeated by Will.

Parents do not inherit from a deceased child if the child was survived by children or lineal descendants. The law has always favored inheritance by lineal descendants over lineal ancestors; descendants being considered of a closer blood relationship than ancestors.

INHERITANCE IF DECEDENT'S SPOUSE SURVIVES

a. **In General**—Although parents always inherit subject to the existing rights of the surviving spouse, many states provide that if a spouse survives, the parents are excluded from inheriting any share of the decedent's estate. If the decedent leaves a surviving spouse in Arizona, Arkansas, Colorado, Florida, Georgia, Illinois, Kansas, Minnesota,

Mississippi, Montana, New Mexico, North Dakota, Ohio, Oregon, Tennessee, Virginia, West Virginia, or Wisconsin, the parents are completely excluded from inheriting any real or personal property. In Arkansas, if the decedent left no descendants and has been continuously married for less than three years, 50% of the estate would pass to the parents in the same manner as if the spouse had not survived the decedent.

Some states allow the spouse to take the whole estate, if it does not exceed a certain value; if the estate exceeds the stated sum, the spouse and parents share proportionately. The sum inherited by the spouse, together with the spouse's share in the excess is as follows: Alabama, $100,000 plus one-half; Alaska, $50,000 plus one-half; Connecticut, $50,000 plus three-quarters; Maine, $50,000 plus one-half; Iowa, $25,000 plus two-thirds; Maryland, $15,000 plus one-half; Massachusetts, $50,000 plus one-half; Michigan, $60,000 plus one-half; Missouri, $20,000 plus one-half; Nebraska, $50,000 plus one-half; New Hampshire, $10,000 plus one-half; Vermont, $25,000 plus one-half; Wyoming, $20,000 plus three-fourths. In California, District of Columbia, Hawaii, Nevada, Oklahoma, and South Carolina, the parents are entitled to one-half the estate if the decedent leaves a spouse surviving. Washington, Ohio, and Indiana allow the parents one-fourth of the estate if a spouse survives.

b. **Personal Property**—In some states parents are not entitled to any personal property if the decedent leaves a surviving spouse. In the following states the surviving spouse inherits all personal property to the exclusion of parents: Illinois, Texas, and Virginia.

In Kentucky parents are only entitled to one-half the decedent's personal property if the spouse survives. Rhode Island allows the surviving spouse $50,000 plus one-half of all personal property, before the parents are entitled to share. In Delaware, the surviving spouse inherits $50,000 plus one-half of the personal property. North Carolina provides that the surviving spouse takes $25,000 plus one-half of the personal property.

c. **Real Property**—Parents may also be excluded from inheriting real property when the decedent leaves a surviving spouse. In Texas and North Carolina the spouse inherits one-half of the decedent's real property before the parents are entitled to share in the decedent's real estate.

INHERITANCE IF BROTHERS AND SISTERS SURVIVE—

Parents, as direct lineal ancestors of the decedent, usually take preference, under the laws of inheritance, over the decedent's brothers and sisters. Under the civil law system of determining heirs, parents stand in the first degree to the decedent and would naturally inherit before the decedent's brothers and sisters, who stand in the second degree.

Parents inherit all real and personal property equally, to the exclusion of the decedents brothers, sisters, and descendants of brothers and sisters in the following states: Alabama, Alaska, Arizona, California, Colorado, Connecticut, Delaware, District of Columbia, Florida, Hawaii, Idaho, Iowa, Kansas, Kentucky, Maine, Maryland, Massachusetts, Michigan, Minnesota, Montana, Nebraska, Nevada, New Hampshire, New Jersey, New Mexico, New York, North Carolina, North Dakota, Ohio, Oklahoma, Oregon, Pennsylvania, Rhode Island, South Dakota, Tennessee, Texas, Utah, Vermont, Virginia, Washington, West Virginia and Wisconsin.

Some states do not follow the general rule, but provide that the parents share in the estate equally with the decedent's brothers, sisters, and deceased brothers and sisters survived by issue. This division of the estate is provided for in Georgia, Mississippi, Missouri, South Carolina, and

Wyoming. In Illinois the parents share equally with the decedent's brothers, sisters, and their descendants; however, if one parent survives, he or she receives a double share. Indiana allows each parent a minimum of one-fourth of the estate if brothers, sisters, or their descendants survive. In Wyoming the parents share with the decedent's brothers, sisters, and descendants; however, if the decedent leaves a surviving spouse, the parents take equally to the exclusion of the decedent's brothers, sisters, and their descendants, that portion of the estate which does not pass to the surviving spouse.

Where no brothers, sisters, or descendants of deceased brothers and sisters survive the decedent, parents inherit the entire estate equally.

INHERITANCE IF ONE PARENT SURVIVES—

Where only one parent survives the decedent, he or she is usually entitled to take the same share that both parents would have taken. In Texas the surviving parent only inherits the same share both parents would take if no brothers, sisters, or their descendants survive the decedent.

Chapter 6

RIGHTS OF BROTHERS, SISTERS AND THEIR DESCENDANTS

IN GENERAL

The decedent's brothers and sisters are generally considered next in line of succession after the decedent's parents. They are collateral kindred, as members of the intestate's immediate family, not in the ascending or descending line of propinquity. As in the case of parents, brothers and sisters do not inherit if the decedent was survived by any lineal descendants; they also take subject to any existing rights of the decedent's spouse.

INHERITANCE IF DECEDENT'S SPOUSE SURVIVES

a. **In General**—If the decedent dies leaving a spouse, brothers and sisters are completely excluded from inheriting any part of the estate in Alabama, Alaska, Arizona, Arkansas, Colorado, Connecticut, Delaware, Florida, Georgia, Hawaii, Idaho, Illinois, Indiana, Kansas, Maine, Maryland, Michigan, Minnesota, Mississippi, Missouri, Montana, Nebraska, New Hampshire, New Jersey, New Mexico, New York, North Carolina, North Dakota, Ohio, Oregon, Pennsylvania, Tennessee, Utah, Virginia, West Virginia, and Wisconsin.

Some states permit brothers and sisters to share the estate with the decedent's spouse. However, in some states the spouse inherits the whole estate up to a states value and one-half of the excess; the remaining one-half being divided among the surviving brothers and sisters and their issue. In Nevada the surviving spouse takes one-half of the separate property, that is, that part of the estate which is not community property. In the following states, the estate must exceed the stated value, before brothers and sisters are entitled to share: Massachusetts, $50,000 and Vermont, $25,000. Wyoming has a similar provision except that the spouse takes $20,000 and three-fourths of the excess, before brothers and sisters are entitled to share.

b. **Personal Property**—In Texas the decedent's brothers and sisters do not inherit any personal property if the decedent's spouse survives. Kentucky allows the brothers and sisters one-half of the personalty, if the spouse survives. Rhode Island allows the surviving spouse $50,000 and one-half of the personal property, before brothers and sisters may share.

c. **Real Property**—Brothers and sisters are limited to an inheritance of one-half of the decedent's real property, in Illinois, Texas, and Washington, if the decedent dies leaving a spouse surviving.

INHERITANCE IF PARENTS SURVIVE—

Brothers and sisters, as collateral relatives of the decedent, are generally not entitled to inherit if the decedent's parents survive. Some states, however, allow brothers and sisters to share with the decedent's parents. In Tennessee only brothers and sisters inherit real property to the exclusion of parents.

Each brother and sister shares equally in the inheritance which passes to them as a group. The estate is divided into as many shares as there are brothers and sisters surviving and deceased brothers and sisters, survived by descendants. If the decedent were survived by two brothers and three sisters, and nieces and nephews who are children of a predeceased brother, the two surviving brothers and three sisters, would each take one sixth of the estate.

INHERITANCE BY REPRESENTATIVES OF DECEASED BROTHERS AND SISTERS:

a. **In General**—Where statutes provide that descendants of deceased brothers and sisters share in the decedent's estate, they receive the same share their parent would have taken. This method of representation is similar to that which is provided for in the case of the decedent's children and lineal descendants. Most states do not allow representation among collateral kindred beyond the children of deceased brothers and sisters. If the decedent was survived by one brother, two sisters, and three children of a predeceased brother, the surviving brother and sisters would each take one fourth of the estate, and the two children of the predeceased brother would take, per stirpes, their deceased parents share of one fourth between them, i.e. each child would take one eighth of the estate.

b. **Nephews and Nieces**—As children of the decedent's brothers and sisters, nephews and nieces are not entitled to inherit, if their parent is alive. If the parent of nephews and nieces predeceased the decedent, they are usually allowed to inherit, by representation, the same share that their parent would have taken. Where there are no brothers and sisters surviving, nieces and nephews inherit equally. They do not represent their deceased parent, but inherit in their own right, and therefore take equally or per capita. In those states which allow representation among collateral kindred beyond the children of brothers and sisters, a grandnephew or grandniece may also inherit with nephews and nieces by representing their predeceased parent. The grandnephews and grandnieces would then take the same share, collectively, that their parent would have taken had he outlived the decedent.

Generally, in order for nephews and nieces to be entitled to inherit, they must be the surviving children of a brother or sister. Nephews and nieces who are children of a brother or sister of the decedent's spouse are not entitled to share in the decedent's estate.

If no brothers and sisters survive the decedent, a problem is presented as to whether the nephews and nieces inherit per stirpes, i.e., the share that their predeceased parent would have taken, or per capita, i.e., each taking an equal share.

Connecticut, and Florida allow lineal descendants of deceased brothers and sisters to take by representation or per stirpes, even though there are no living brothers or sisters, and those entitled to inherit stand in equal degree. In many states, however, nephews and nieces inherit equally or per capita, if no brothers and sisters survive the decedent; they take in their own right, and not by representation.

In some states there is a provision in the inheritance laws that the estate shall pass to the decedent's brothers, sisters, and descendants of deceased brothers and sisters. In Maine, if no brothers and sisters survive, nieces and nephews inherit per capita, as next of kin, and not as representatives of the predeceased brothers and sisters.

Although nieces and nephews are mentioned in the general provision for inheritance by brothers, sisters and their descendants, statutes may provide that if the decedent is not survived by a spouse, descendants, parents, brothers or sisters, the estate shall pass to the next of kin. In such cases, nephews and nieces will always share equally or per capita, as next of kin.

Chapter 7

RIGHTS OF OTHER RELATIVES

IN GENERAL—

The inheritance rights of the decedent's relatives, other than his spouse, parents, brothers, sisters, and their descendants, can generally be classified into two general types. In most states the law enumerates the share or amount inherited by the spouse, parents, brothers, sisters, and their descendants, and then provides that the estate shall pass to the next-of-kin in equal degree. Other states provide that the estate shall be divided into moieties or equal parts, and in the absence of a surviving spouse, parent, brother, sister, or their descendants, one moiety passes to the maternal kindred and the other to the paternal kindred. The remaining states have varied provisions affecting the inheritance rights of the decedent's relatives.

Inheritance is based, primarily, on the closeness of relationship to the decedent; however, this relationship can be either lineal or collateral. Although this chapter will only discuss the inheritance rights of relatives other than the decedent's spouse, parents, brothers, sisters, and their descendants, it is important that the consanguinity or relationship between all blood relations be generally considered.

Although the degrees of relationship may be easily determined, it must be noted that the next-of-kin as determined by their relationship to the decedent are only entitled to inherit if the decedent is not survived by any persons specifically mentioned by the statute as being entitled to share in the estate. If the statutes allow the decedent's nephews and nieces to inherit after brothers and sisters, but before the estate passes to the next-of-kin, nephews and nieces will inherit to the exclusion of aunts and uncles, although they all stand in the same degree of relationship to the decedent.

Many states have statutes similar to that of Massachusetts which provides that: "If he (the intestate) leaves no issue and no father, mother, brother or sister and no issue of any deceased brother or sister, then to the next of kin in equal degree; but if there are two or more collateral kindred in equal degree claiming through different ancestors, those claiming through the nearest ancestor shall be preferred to those claiming through an ancestor more remote." (ch.190 §3). Under this provision, if the only surviving relatives were a first cousin and a grand-uncle, the first cousin would inherit to the exclusion of the grand-uncle even though both are related to the decedent in the fourth degree. Both claimants are related to the decedent through ancestors; however, the relationship between the first cousin and the decedent stems from the decedent's grandfather, while the relationship between the decedent and his grand-uncle stems from the former's great-grandfather.

When entitled to inherit, next-of-kin each take an equal share. There is generally no right of representation among collaterals beyond descendants of deceased brothers and sisters; therefore, if the decedent was survived by two cousins and children of a predeceased cousin, the two surviving cousins would share equally to the exclusion of the predeceased cousin's surviving children. An exception to the general rule may be found in the Delaware law which allows the issue of predeceased next-of-kin to inherit by representation the same share their predeceased parent would have taken had he outlived the decedent.

The following chart is based on the Standardized Genealogical Consanguinity Chart prepared by John Reynold Totten for the New York Genealogical and Biographical Society, and illustrates various degrees of relationship under the Civil law.

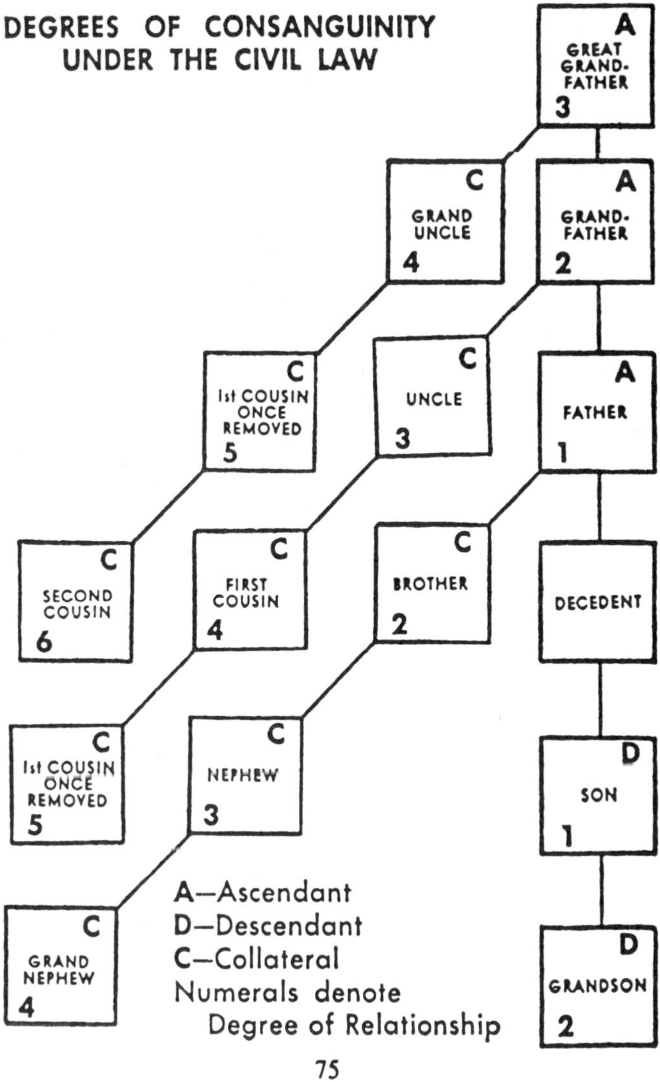

COMPUTATION OF KINDRED—

The states which provide that the estate shall pass to the next-of-kin in equal degree, generally follow the Civil law method in determining degrees of consanguinity. According to the Civil law, degrees of blood relationship between collaterals are determined by counting from the decedent up to the common ancestor and then down to the claimant; the total being the degree of relationship.

The states which provide that the estate shall pass to grandparents or other ancestors and then down to their descendants generally follow the parentelic system or Canons of Descent. Under this scheme, if there are no lineal descendants, the nearest ascendants take, and then their issue to the remotest degree, upon failure of such heirs, the estate passes to the next nearest ancestors and their descendants.

Many states have a mixed system of descent and distribution, combining the parentelic system by enumerating the ancestors who are entitled to share and, in the absence of such persons, providing that the estate shall pass to the next of kin as determined under the Civil law.

IF DECEDENT'S SPOUSE SURVIVES—

As in the case of brothers, sisters and parents, the decedent's other relatives always inherit subject to the existing rights of the decedent's spouse. In most states, if a spouse survives, next-of-kin are completely excluded from any inheritance. In South Carolina the decedent's relatives may only share in one-half of the estate if a spouse survives. Vermont allows the spouse $25,000 plus one-half of the excess if the decedent leaves kindred surviving. In Massachusetts the estate must exceed $50,000 before the kindred are entitled to share.

Some states restrict the share which the kindred may inherit in personal property, if a spouse survives. Rhode Island allows either spouse an inheritance in personal property of

$50,000 and one-half of the excess, before kindred may inherit. Kentucky only allows the decedent's kindred to share in one-half of the decedent's personal property if a spouse survives.

ANCESTRAL PROPERTY—

Where the decedent dies leaving property which he acquired by gift, devise or descent from his parent or other ancestor, many states provide that the property shall pass to the descendants of the parent from whom he received the property, to the exclusion of the other parent's relatives. Under this provision, if the decedent died leaving ancestral property received from his predeceased father and he was survived by two uncles, one of whom was his father's brother and the other his mother's brother, the property would pass to his father's brother, and his other uncle would take nothing. The statutes may provide a point or limit of kindred relationship beyond which the exclusion provision will not be given effect. In Kentucky, ancestral property received from one parent descends to that parent and his kindred, and if none, then to the other parent and his kindred; the law also provides that the kindred of one parent shall not be excluded by the kindred of the other parent, if the latter is more remote than the grandfather, grandmother, uncles and aunts of the intestate and their descendants (§391.020).

GRANDPARENTS AND OTHER ANCESTORS—

a. As **next-of-kin**—In the majority of states where the next-of-kin are entitled to inherit if the decedent is not survived by a spouse, parent, brother, sister, or other descendants, grandparents will inherit equally to the exclusion of other relatives related in a more remote degree. Great-grandparents may also inherit equally as next of kin, if the decedent is not survived by relatives more closely related.

As next-of-kin, there is no distinction made between maternal and paternal grandparents or ancestors. Where grandparents or great-grandparents are entitled to inherit as next-of-kin, they share equally with those related in the same degree, except in those states which provide that those claiming through the nearest lineal ancestor exclude those of a more remote ancestor. In that case, a grandparent would exclude the decedent's uncle; however, the decedent's uncle would exclude the decedent's great-grandfather although both are related in the third degree.

b. **Maternal and Paternal Kindred**—Some states provide that in the absence of closer relatives, the estate shall be divided into two equal parts or moieties and pass to the decedent's maternal and paternal kindred. The division of the estate from this point varies somewhat in many states.

In Texas and West Virginia, one moiety or share passes to the grandparents if both are living; however, if only one is alive, he takes only one-half, and the other one-half passes to the deceased grandparent's descendants, namely the decedent's uncles, aunts, and their descendants. In Florida, Kentucky, Ohio, Rhode Island, and Virginia, the law also provides that the estate be divided into moities; however, the grandparents share equally, and if only one survives, he or she inherits the entire moiety before the descendant's aunts, uncles and their descendants are entitled to share.

In those instances where the decedent leaves only maternal or paternal kindred but not both, the entire estate then passes to the surviving line.

c. **Sharing with uncles, aunts and their descendants**—Although grandparents may not always inherit to the exclusion of the decedent's uncles and aunts, some states provide that they may all share equally in the estate. In Colorado, Missouri, and Wyoming, the decedent's grandmother, grandfather, uncles, aunts, and descendants of deceased uncles and aunts each take an equal share, inheriting as members of a single class. The estate is divided into as many shares as there are grandparents, uncles, aunts, and predeceased uncles and aunts survived by descendants. No distinction is made between the maternal and paternal relatives.

In Iowa, the share which would have passed to the decedent's parents had they not predeceased him passes as if they had outlived him. Therefore, the grandparents inherit the same share the decedent's parents would have taken. Kansas has a similar rule, in that the property passes to the parents' heirs in the same manner as if the parents had predeceased the decedent.

d. **Great Grandparents**—In those states which provide for a division of the estate between the maternal and paternal kindred, great-grandparents are entitled to inherit in the same manner, and to the same extent, as grandparents. If, therefore, there are no grandparents, uncles, aunts, or descendants of deceased uncles and aunts, the great-grandparents take the same share as the grandparents would have taken and either exclude or share with the decedent's great-uncles and great-aunts and their descendants.

UNCLES AND AUNTS

a. **As next-of-kin**—Aunts and uncles will inherit equally, if there are no persons more closely related to the decedent, in those states which provide that the estate shall pass to the next-of-kin in equal degree in the absence of persons specifically enumerated in the statute. Where uncles and aunts are so entitled to inherit, both paternal and maternal uncles and aunts inherit equally. As next-of-kin, they usually do not inherit to the exclusion of descendants of deceased brothers and sisters. In the states which provide that the next-of-kin of the nearest ancestor inherit to the exclusion of those claiming through a more remote ancestor, they will inherit to the exclusion of the great-grandparents although they are both related in the third degree of a kindred.

b. **Maternal and Paternal Kindred**—In states where the estate is divided into moieties, between the paternal and maternal kindred, some states allow the uncles and aunts to share equally with the grandparents, while others only permit them to take if no grandparents survive. In either case, however, the descendants of predeceased uncles and aunts are entitled to share with the surviving uncles and aunts.

COUSINS—

As next-of-kin, cousins are entitled to inherit in the absence of those of a closer degree of relationship to the decedent. First cousins are related in the fourth degree and usually take to the exclusion of first cousins-once-removed who stand in the fifth degree or second cousins who are related in the sixth degree. Cousins usually share equally and take to the exclusion of descendants of predeceased cousins. Although most states do not allow representation among remote collaterals, Delaware permits descendants of predeceased cousins to share per stirpes with surviving cousins.

Cousins may share equally with other relatives related in the same degree. If the decedent is survived by a first cousin and a grand-uncle, each would take a like share, being equally related to the decedent in the fourth degree. The first cousin would take the entire estate, however, if the state law provides that the estate shall pass to those claiming through the nearest ancestor to the exclusion of those claiming through a more remote ancestor.

HALF-BLOODS:

a. **In General**—The term "whole blood" is defined as the blood or relationship of children who have both their parents in common; and "half-blood" is defined as the relationship between children who have at least one of the parents in common. Under the common law, property did not pass to those related by half-blood. The modern tendency is toward abolishing any distinction between persons of half-blood and those of whole-blood.

At the present time, kindred related by half-blood inherit equally with those of whole-blood in the following states: Alabama, Alaska, Arizona, Arkansas, Colorado, Delaware, Georgia, Idaho, Illinois, Indiana, Iowa, Maine, Maryland,

Massachusetts, Michigan, Montana, Nebraska, New Jersey, New York, North Carolina, North Dakota, Ohio, Oregon, Pennsylvania, Rhode Island, Tennessee, Vermont, West Virginia, Wisconsin and the District of Columbia. Although Kansas has no statutory provision, it has been held that children of half-blood inherit equally with those of whole-blood (136 Kan. 228 (1932)).

Some states only permit half-blood to inherit one-half as much as the share taken by kindred of the whole-blood, providing they all stand in equal degree. This rule is followed by the laws of Florida, Kentucky, Missouri, Texas, Virginia and West Virginia.

In Connecticut and Mississippi kindred of the whole-blood take to the exclusion of those of half-blood of equal degree.

In Wyoming, although no distinction is made between children of whole or half-blood, collaterals of half-blood only inherit one-half the share taken by those of whole-blood standing in equal degree. California permits kindred of half-blood to inherit to the exclusion of those of whole-blood standing in a more remote degree.

b. **Ancestral Property**—The inheritance laws of some states provide that kindred of the half-blood inherit equally with those of the whole-blood in equal degree, unless the property was obtained by gift, devise or descent from one of the decedent's ancestors. The states so providing are as follows: Alabama, California, Hawaii, Michigan, Minnesota, Nebraska, Nevada, Oklahoma, South Dakota, Tennessee, Utah, and Washington. The statutes may permit half-bloods to inherit ancestral property if they are of the blood of the ancestor. In other words, if they are directly related by blood to the ancestor from or through whom the property passed.

Chapter 8

ALIENS

INHERITANCE UNDER STATE LAW—

At common law aliens could not take real property by inheritance even though they could acquire it by purchase or devise. Statutes have since been passed in most states removing the common law disability and allowing inheritance by and from aliens in the same manner and to the same extent as citizens.

In some states, there are statutes which discriminate against certain classes of aliens in the matter of continuing to hold property acquired by inheritance. Illinois permits aliens to hold property for six years, at the end of which time they must either convey or become citizens.

Some state statutes restrict the privilege of inheritance to resident aliens or those who are nationals of countries friendly to the United States. A few states permit aliens who have declared their intention to become citizens to have the same rights as citizens to the extent of being able to possess and transmit property by inheritance.

At common law, an alien was not restricted from inheriting personal property. Most states continue to recognize the alien's right to inherit personalty; however, in some cases, where a restricted right to take real property exists, the right to inherit personalty may also be restricted. Where the law permits an alien to inherit "property", it usually means both real and personal property.

INHERITANCE UNDER TREATY PROVISION

The United States, under the treaty making power, has entered into many agreements with foreign countries concerning an alien's right to take, hold, and transmit property. Although it is the settled law in this country that a state may lawfully prohibit aliens from owning or acquiring any lands within its borders, a state may only so act in the absence of a treaty to the contrary.

The treaties which have been entered into by the United States with foreign countries are usually reciprocal, allowing aliens the same rights to inherit property that are granted to citizens of the United States in that foreign country. Although the alien is thus afforded certain rights, in most instances, state laws give aliens even greater property rights than those granted under a treaty. In remarkably few treaties is there to be found a provision granting aliens in our country or to our citizens in foreign countries all the property rights possessed by the nationals of the respective countries.

SUMMARY OF STATE LAWS*

ALABAMA

No person is disqualified to take as an heir because he or a person through whom he claims is or has been an alien (§2-112).

ALASKA

No person is disqualified to take as an heir because he or a person through whom he claims is or has been an alien (§13. 11.060).

ARIZONA

No person is disqualified to take as an heir because he

*See Table of Statutory References.

or a person through whom he claims is or has been an alien (§14.2112).

ARKANSAS

Resident aliens may inherit property the same as citizens (Constitution, Art. II, §20). All real property owned by an alien passes on his death in the same manner as property owned by citizens (§50-301). Personal property owned by a resident alien is distributed in the same manner as if he were a citizen (§61-106).

CALIFORNIA

Any person, whether citizen or alien, may take and dispose of real or personal property (C.C. §671).

COLORADO

No person is disqualified to take as an heir because he or a person through whom he claims is or has been an alien (§152-2-112).

CONNECTICUT

Resident aliens may inherit and transmit real estate in the manner and to the same extent as citizens (§47-57).

DELAWARE

All real and personal property located in the state may be inherited by and through an alien in the same manner as by a citizen of the state (T.25 §§306,307).

DELAWARE

All real and personal property located in the state may be inherited by and through an alien in the same manner as by a citizen of the state (T.25 §§306,307). No person is disqualified to take as an heir because he or a person through whom he claims is or has been an alien (T.12 §507).

DISTRICT OF COLUMBIA

Aliens are entitled to inherit realty to the same extent as citizens (U.S.C. Tit. 48, §1508). A good title by descent may be derived by those claiming through an alien ancestor (T.19 §321)

FLORIDA

No person is disqualified to take as an heir because he, or a person through whom he claims is, or has been, an alien. (§732.1101)

GEORGIA

Aliens, subjects of governments at peace with the United States, shall be entitled to all the rights of citizens of other states resident in this state (§32-2-4).

HAWAII

No person is disqualified to take as an heir because he or a person through whom he claims is or has been an alien (§560:2-112).

IDAHO

No person is disqualified to take as an heir because he or a person through whom he claims is or has been an alien (§15-2-112).

ILLINOIS

All aliens may inherit and transmit real property by inheritance. No person shall be deprived of his right to inherit real property from any deceased person because he may be an alien or be compelled to trace his relationship to such deceased person through one or more aliens (Ch. 6, §1). An alien may not hold property for more than six years, at which time he must convey or become a citizen of the United States, (Ch. 6, §2). All aliens may acquire and hold personal property in the same manner as citizens of the United States (Ch. 6, §7).

INDIANA

All aliens residing in the state who have declared their intention to become citizens of the United States may acquire and hold real estate in the same manner as citizens (32-1-7-1). All aliens may inherit real estate except that holding in excess of 320 acres will escheat to the state if not conveyed within five years unless the owner becomes a U.S. citizen within that time (32-1-8-1, 2).

IOWA

Resident aliens enjoy the same rights in respect to descent of property as native-born citizens (Const., Art. I, §22). Non-resident aliens may acquire by demise or descent real property, except agricultural land as hereinafter noted, and may hold, devise an alienate real property (§567.1). A non-resident alien acquiring an interest in agricultural land shall divest himself of all interest in the land within two years from the date of acquiring such interest. However such divestment is not required if the interest was acquired by devise or descent from a non-resident alien if such interest was acquired by any non-resident alien prior to July 1, 1979. Restrictions set forth do not apply where land does not exceed 320 acres acquired for use other than farming (§567).

KANSAS

All aliens eligible to citizenship under the law of the United States may transmit and inherit real estate in this state in the same manner and to the same extent as citizens of the United States (§59-511). Other aliens may only inherit to the same extent as provided in the treaty between the United States and the alien's country (§59-512). Whenever an alien heir or devisee cannot take real estate, the court will order a sale and distribute the proceeds to the alien in lieu of such property.

KENTUCKY

Any alien, not an enemy, after declaring his intention to become a citizen of the United States, may inherit any interest in real or personal property, in the same manner as if he were a citizen of this state (§381.290). If real estate passes to a non-resident alien by descent, such property may be held and alienated by such alien for eight years after the final settlement of the decedent's estate (§381.330). An alien may inherit personal property in the same manner as a citizen (§391.030). A person may inherit even though the ancestor through whom he claims is an alien (§391.060).

LOUISIANA

Aliens may inherit both real and personal property.

MAINE

No person is disqualified to take as an heir because he or a person through whom he claims is or has been an alien (18-A §2-112).

MARYLAND

Aliens, not enemies, may inherit and transmit by inheritance real property in the same manner as citizens (§14-101).

MASSACHUSETTS

Aliens may take and transmit real property, and no title to real property shall be invalid on account of the alienage of a former owner (Ch. 184 §1).

MICHIGAN

Any alien may acquire and hold real property by inheritance, and if he shall die intestate, his realty descends to his heirs; and in all cases realty passes in the same manner as if such alien were a native citizen (§554.135).

MINNESOTA

Aliens may inherit real property in the same manner as citizens (§500.22).

MISSISSIPPI

Resident aliens may acquire, hold, and transmit real property by descent, as citizens of the state may (§89-1-23).

MISSOURI

Aliens are capable of acquiring by descent, real estate, and of alienating the same as if they were citizens of the United States and residents of the state (§442.560).

MONTANA

No person is disqualified to take as an heir because he or a person through whom he claims is an alien unless the country in which he resides does not allow reciprocity (§72-2-214).

NEBRASKA

Aliens may not hold any land for more than five years (§76-402), except that a resident alien may acquire land by inheritance, provided that he shall sell the same within five years from the date of acquiring, and if he fails to do so, the property escheats to the state (§76-405). Nebraska has adopted the Uniform Probate Code effective January 1, 1977. The Code provides that no person is disqualified to take as an heir because he or a person through whom he claims is or has been an alien except as provided in §4-107 and §76-4.

NEVADA

Any nonresident alien may take, hold, and enjoy any real property within the state the same as any resident citizen (§111-055). However, the rights of aliens not residing within the United States to take real or personal property by inheritance are dependent in each case upon the existence of a reciprocal right upon the parts of citizens of the United States to take real and personal property in like manner within the countries of which said aliens are inhabitants or citizens (§134-230).

NEW HAMPSHIRE

An alien, resident in this state, may take, hold or devise real estate; and it may descend in the same manner as if he were a citizen (Ch. 477 §20).

NEW JERSEY

Alien friends have the same rights with respect to real property as native-born citizens (T.46, §3-18). A person is not disqualified to take as an heir because he or a person through whom he claims is or has been an alien (T. 3B §5-12).

NEW MEXICO

Aliens have full power and authority to acquire or hold real estate by deed, Will, inheritance or otherwise and also to alienate, sell, assign and tranfer the same to their heirs or other persons whether such heirs or other prsons are, or are not, citizens of the United States. When an alien having title or interest in any lands or estate dies, such lands of estate shall descend and vest in the same manner as if such alien were a citizen of the United States (§45-2-112). Unless otherwise provided by law, no alien, ineligible to citizenship, shall acquire title, leasehold or other interest in or to real estate in New Mexico (Const. Art. II, §22).

NEW YORK

Aliens are empowered to take, hold, transmit, and dispose of real property within this state in the same manner as native-born citizens and their heirs and devisees take in the same manner as citizens (R.P.L., §10).

NORTH CAROLINA

Resident aliens may inherit and transmit real property in the same manner as citizens (§64-1). Nonresident aliens may only inherit if a reciprocal right exists in the citizens or residents of the United States(§64-3). Unless otherwise provided, it shall be no bar to intestate succession by any person that he, or any person through whom he traces his inheritance is or has been an alien (§29-11).

NORTH DAKOTA

No person is disqualified to take as an heir because he or a person through whom he claims is or has been an alien (§30.1 -04-12).

OHIO

No person capable of inheriting shall be deprived of an inheritance by reason of the alienage of any of his ancestors. Aliens may hold realty by descent as fully and completely as any citizen of the United States (§2105.16).

OKLAHOMA

Aliens may take in all cases, by succession, as well as citizens; and no person is precluded from such succession by reason of the alienage of any relative (T. 84, §229). However, nonresident aliens may only hold title to real estate for five years (T. 60 §123).

OREGON

No special statutory provision.

PENNSYLVANIA

Real and personal estate shall pass without regard to whether the decedent or any person otherwise entitled to take is, or has been, an alien (T.20, §1.4 (7)).

RHODE ISLAND

Aliens may take, hold, and transmit real and personal property in the same manner as citizens (§34-2-1). Where it appears that a nonresident alien would not have the benefit or control of his inheritance, the probate court may direct that such inheritance be paid into the registry of the probate court for the nonresident's benefit. (§33-13-13).

SOUTH CAROLINA

Real and personal property may be acquired and disposed of by an alien in the same manner and in all respects as by a natural born citizen, and title to real and personal may be derived from, through, or in succession to an alien, in the same manner, in all respects, as though, from or in succession to a natural born citizen (§27-23-10). Except that aliens or corporations controlled by aliens may not own or control more than 500,000 acres of land within the state

(§27-13-30). Alien widows of United States citizens have the same property rights as citizens (§21-1-40).

SOUTH DAKOTA

Aliens may inherit and transmit property in this state and dispose of or transmit the same as a citizen, and no person is precluded from inheriting by reason of the alienage of any relative (§29-1-17). No distinction shall ever be made between aliens and citizens in reference to descent of property (Const., Art. II §14).

TENNESSEE

An alien, resident or nonresident of the United States may take and hold real and personal property in this state and dispose of or transmit the same as a native citizen (§64-201). The heirs of such aliens may take by inheritance as if citizens of the United States (§64-202).

TEXAS

No person is disqualified to take as an heir because he or a person through whom he claims is or has been an alien (§41 (c)).

UTAH

Aliens may, in all cases, take by succession and no person is precluded from inheriting by reason of the alienage of any relatives (§74-4-24).

VERMONT

Aliens, not enemies, may acquire real or personal property the same as citizens (25 Vt. 433).

VIRGINIA

Any alien, not an enemy, may acquire and transmit real estate by descent in the same manner as property held by citizens (§55-1). In taking title by descent, it is no bar to a party that any ancestor through whom he inherits is, or has been, an alien (§64.1-4).

WASHINGTON

Any alien may acquire and hold lands, or any right thereto, or interest therein, by purchase, demise or descent; and he may convey, mortgage and devise the same, and if he shall die intestate, the same shall descend to his heirs, and in all cases such lands shall be held, conveyed, mortgaged or devised, or shall descend in like manner and with like effect as if such alien were a native citizen of this state or of the United States (§64.16.005).

WEST VIRGINIA

Any alien may take by devise, inheritance, gift or purchase, and hold, convey, devise or otherwise dispose of land within the State as if he were a citizen, and if an alien owner of land within this State shall die, his land shall descend in the same manner as if he were a citizen (§36-1-21). In making title by descent, it shall be no bar to a party that any ancestor, whether living or dead, through whom he derives his descent from the intestate is or has been an alien (§42-1-4).

WISCONSIN

Aliens may inherit and transmit by inheritance in the same manner and to the same extent as citizens (§710.01).

WYOMING

Resident aliens may inherit and transmit property the same as citizens (Const., Art. 1, §29). The alienage of the legal heirs shall not invalidate any title to real estate which shall descend or pass from the decedent except that no nonresident alien who is a citizen of any country foreign to the United States of America, shall by any manner or means acquire real property in this state by succession or testamentary disposition if the laws of the country of which such nonresident alien is a citizen do not allow citizens of the United States of America to take real property by succession or by testamentary disposition (§2-4-105).

Chapter 9

UNIFORM PROBATE CODE

IN GENERAL

The Uniform Probate Code was approved by the National Conference of Commissioners on Uniform State Laws and by the American Bar Association in August 1969. The underlying purposes and policies of the Code include the simplification and clarification of the law concerning the affairs of decedents, protected persons, minors, and to discover and make effective the intent of a decedent in the distribution of his property (U.P.C. §1-102).

The Code has been adopted by Alaska (effective January 1, 1973); Arizona (effective January 1, 1974), Colorado (effective July 1, 1974) Florida (effective July 1, 1975), Hawaii (effective July 1, 1976, Idaho (effective July 1, 1972), Maine (effective January 1, 1981), Michigan (effective July 1, 1979), Minnesota (effective August 1, 1975), Montana (effective July 1, 1975), Nebraska (effective January 1, 1977), New Mexico (effective July 1, 1976), North Dakota (effective July 1, 1975), Utah (effective July 1, 1977). New Jersey did not adopt the code, as such, but enacted legislation similar to the Code provisions. Alabama adopted a new Law of Intestate Succession effective January 1, 1983 using the Code as a guide. However the Alabama law has many material differences from the Code.

The author and publisher of this work extend grateful acknowledgement to the National Conference of Commissioners on Uniform State Laws for permission to reproduce portions of the Official Text and Comments for the Uniform Probate Code.

OFFICIAL TEXT AND COMMENTS APPROVED BY THE NATIONAL CONFERENCE OF COMMISSIONERS ON UNIFORM STATE LAWS

AN ACT

Relating to affairs of decedents, missing persons, protected persons, minors, incapacitated persons and certain others and constituting the Uniform Probate Code; consolidating and revising aspects of the law relating to Wills and intestacy and the administration and distribution of estates of decedents, missing persons, protected persons, minors, incapacitated persons and certain others; ordering the powers and procedures of the Court concerned with the affairs of decedents and certain others; providing for the validity and effect of certain non-testamentary transfers, contracts and deposits which relate to death and appear to have testamentary effect; providing certain procedures to facilitate enforcement of testatmentary and other trusts; making uniform the law with respect to decedents and certain others; and repealing inconsistent legislation.

COMMENT

The long title of the Code should be adapted to the constitutional, statutory requirements and practices of the enacting state. The concept of the Code is that the "affairs of decedents, missing persons, disabled persons, minors, and certain others" is a single subject of the law notwithstanding its many facets.

UNIFORM PROBATE CODE
ARTICLE II
PART I
INTESTATE SUCCESSION

PART 2
ELECTIVE SHARE OF SURVIVING SPOUSE

PART 3
SPOUSE AND CHILDREN UNPROVIDED FOR IN WILLS

PART 4
EXEMPT PROPERTY AND ALLOWANCES

PART 1

INTESTATE SUCCESSION

GENERAL COMMENT

Part 1 of Article II contains the basic pattern of intestate succession historically called descent and distribution. It is no longer meaningful to have different patterns for real and personal property, and under the proposed statute all property not disposed of by a decedent's will passes to his heirs in the same manner. The existing statutes on descent and distribution in the United States vary from state to state. The most common pattern for the immediate family retains the imprint of history, giving the widow a third of realty (sometimes only for life by her dower right) and a third of the personalty, with the balance passing to issue. Where the decedent is survived by no issue, but leaves a spouse and collateral blood relatives, there is wide variation in disposition of the intestate estate, some states giving all to the surviving spouse, some giving substantial shares to the blood relatives. The Code attempts to reflect the normal desire of the owner of wealth as to disposition of his property at death, and for this purpose the prevailing patterns in wills are useful in determining what the owner who fails to execute a will would probably want.

A principal purpose of this Article and Article III of the Code is to provide suitable rules and procedures for the person of modest means who relies on the estate plan provided by law. For a discussion of this important aspect of the Code, see 3 Real Property, Probate and Trust Journal (Fall 1968) P. 199.

The principal features of Part 1 are:

(1) A larger share is given to the surviving spouse, if there are issue, and the whole estate is there are no issue or parent.

(2) Inheritance by collateral relatives is limited to grand-

parents and those descended from grandparents. This simplifies proof of heirship and eliminates will contests by remote relatives.

(3) An heir must survive the decedent for five days in order to take under the statute. This is an extension of the reasoning behind the Uniform Simultaneous Death Act and is similar to provisions found in many wills.

(4) Adopted children are treated as children of the adopting parents for all inheritance purposes and cease to be children of natural parents; this reflects modern policy of recent statutes and court decisions.

(5) In an era when inter vivos gifts are frequently made within the family, it is unrealistic to preserve concepts of advancement developed when such gifts were rare. The statute provides that gifts during lifetime are not advancements unless declared or acknowledged in writing.

While the prescribed patterns may strike some as rules of law which may in some cases defeat intent of a decedent, this is true of every statute of this type. In assessing the changes it must therefore be borne in mind that the decedent may always choose a different rule by executing a will.

Section 2-101. Intestate Estate.

Any part of the estate of a decedent not effectively disposed of by his will passes to his heirs as prescribed in the following sections of this Code.

Section 2-102. Share of the Spouse.

The intestate share of the surviving spouse is:

(1) if there is no surviving issue or parent of the decedent, the entire intestate estate;

(2)if there is no surviving issue but the decedent is survived by a parent or parents, the first ($50,000), plus one-half of the balance of the intestate estate;

(3) if there are surviving issue all of whom are issue of the surviving spouse also, the first ($50,000), plus one-half of the balance of the intestate estate;

(4) if there are surviving issue one or more of whom are not issue of the surviving spouse, one-half of the intestate estate.

COMMENT

This section gives the surviving spouse a larger share than most existing statutes on descent and distribution. In doing so, it reflects the desires of most married persons, who almost always leave all of a moderate estate or at least one-half of a larger estate to the surviving spouse when a will is executed. A husband or wife who desires to leave the surviving spouse less than the share provided by this section may do so by executing a will, subject of course to possible election by the surviving spouse to take an elective share of one-third under Part 2 of this Article. Moreover, in the small estate (less than $50,000 after homestead allowance, exempt property, and allowances) the surviving spouse is given the entire estate if there are only children who are issue of both the decedent and the surviving spouse; the result is to avoid protective proceedings as to property otherwise passing to their minor children. See Section 2-802 for the definition of spouse which controls for purposes of intestate succession.

ALTERNATIVE PROVISION FOR COMMUNITY PROPERTY STATES

Section 2-102A. Share of the Spouse.

The intestate share of the surviving spouse is as follows:

(1) as to separate property

(i) if there is no surviving issue or parent of the decedent, the entire intestate estate;

(ii) if there is no surviving issue but the decedent is survived by a parent or parents, the first ($50,000), plus one-half of the balance of the intestate estate;

(iii) if there are surviving issue all of whom are issue of the surviving spouse also, the first ($50,000), plus one-half of the balance of the intestate estate;

(iv) if there are surviving issue one or more of whom are not issue of the surviving spouse, one-half of the intestate estate.

(2) as to community property

(i) The one-half of community property which belongs to the decedent passes to the (surviving spouse).

Section 2-103. Share of Heirs Other Than Surviving Spouse.

The part of the intestate estate not passing to the surviving spouse under Section 2-102, or the entire intestate estate if there is no surviving spouse, passes as follows:

(1) to the issue of the decedent; if they are all of the same degree of kinship to the decedent, they take equally, but if of unequal degree, then those of more remote degree take by representation;

(2) if there is no surviving issue, to his parent or parents equally;

(3) if there is no surviving issue or parent, to the brothers and sisters and the issue of each deceased brother or sister by representation; if there is no surviving brother or sister, the issue of brothers and sisters take equally if they are all of the same degree of kinship to the decedent, but if of unequal degree then those of more remote degree take by representation;

(4) if there is no surviving issue, parent or issue of a parent, but the decedent is survived by one or more grandparents or issue of grandparents, half of the estate passes to the paternal grandparents if both survive, or to the surviving paternal grandparent, or to the issue.of the paternal grandparents if

both are deceased, the issue taking equally if they are all of the same degree of kinship to the decedent, but if of unequal degree those of more remote degree take by representation; and the other half passes to the maternal relatives in the same manner; but if there be no surviving grandparent or issue of grandparent on either the paternal or the maternal side, the entire estate passes to the relatives on the other side in the same manner as the half.

COMMENT

This section provides for inheritance by lineal descendants of the decedent, parents and their descendants, and grandparents and collateral relatives descended from grandparents. In line with modern policy, it eliminates more remote relatives tracing through great-grandparents.

In general the principle of representation (which is defined in Section 2-106) is adopted as the pattern which most decedents would prefer.

If the pattern of this section is not desired, it may be avoided by a properly executed will or, after the decedent's death, by renunciation by particular heirs under Section 2-801.

In 1975, the Joint Editorial Board recommended replacement of the original text of subsection (3) which referred to "brothers and sisters" of the decedent, and to their issue. The new language is much simpler, and it avoids the problem that "brother" and "sister" are not defined terms. "Issue" by contrast is defined in Section 1-201 (21). The definition refers to other defined terms, "parent" and "child", both of which refer to Section 2-109 where the effect of illegitimacy and adoption on relationship for inheritance purposes is spelled out.

The Joint Editorial Board gave careful consideration to a change in the Code's system for distribution among issue as recommended in Waggoner, "A Proposed Alternative to the Uniform Probate Code's System for Intestate Distribution Among Descendants," 66 Nw. U.L. Rev. 626 (1971). Though favored as a recommended change in the Code by a majority of the Board, others opposed on the ground that the original text had been enacted already in several states, and that a change in this basic section of the Code would weaken the case for uniformity of probate law in all states. Nonetheless, since some states as of 1975 had adopted versions of the Code containing deviations from the original text of this and related sections, it was the consensus that Prof. Waggoner's recommendation and the statutory changes that would be necessary to implement it, should be described in Code commentary.

The changes involved would appear in this section and in Section 2-106. The old and the revised text of these sections would be as follows if the Waggoner recommendation is accepted by an enacting state which decides that uniformity of the substantive rules of intestate succession is not vital:

Change Section 2-103(1), (3) and (4) by altering, in each instance, the language referring to taking per capita or by representation, as follows:

2-103 . . .

(1) to the issue of the decedent; *to be distributed per capita at each generation as defined in Section 2-106;* if they are all of the same degree of kinship to the decedent they take equally, but if of unequal degree then those of more remote degree take by representation;

(3) if there is no surviving issue or parent, to the issue of the parents or either of them *to be distributed per capita at each generation as defind in Section 2-106;* by representation;

(4) . . . or to the issue of the paternal grandparents if both are deceased *to be distributed per capita at each generation as defined in Section 2-106;* the issue taking equally if they are all of the same degree of kinship to the decedent, but if of unequal degree those of more remote degree take by representation.

Also, alter 2-106 as follows:

SECTION 2-106. *[Per Capita at Each Generation.]*

If per capita at each generation representation is called for by this Code, the estate is divided into as many shares as there are surviving heirs in the nearest degree of kinship *which contains any surviving heirs* and deceased persons in the same degree who left issue who survive the decedent. Each surviving heir in the nearest degree *which contains any surviving heir is allocated one share and the remainder of the estate is divided in the same manner as if the heirs already allocated a share and their issue had predeceased the decedent.* receiving one share and the share of each deceased person in the same degree being divided among his issue in the same manner.

Section 2-104. Requirement That Heir Survive Decedent For 120 Hours.

Any person who fails to survive the decedent by 120 hours is deemed to have predeceased the decedent for purposes of homestead allowance, exempt property, and intestate succession, and the decedent's heirs are determined accordingly. If the time of death of the decedent or of the person who would otherwise be an heir, or the times of death of both, cannot be determined, and it cannot be established that the person who would otherwise be an heir has survived the decedent by 120 hours, it is deemed that the person failed to survive for the required period.This section is not to be applied where its application would result in a taking of intestate estate by the state under Section 2-105.

COMMENT

This section is a limited version of the type of clause frequently found in wills to take care of the common accident situation, in which several members of the same family are injured and die within a few days of each other. The Uniform Simultaneous Death Act provides only a partial solution, since it applies only if there is no proof that the parties died otherwise than simultaneously. This section requires an heir to survive by five days in order to succeed to decedent's intestate property; for a comparable provision as to wills, see Section 2-601. This section avoids multiple administrations and in some instances prevents the property from passing to persons not desired by the decedent. The five-day period will not hold up administration of a decedent's estate because sections 3-302 and 3-307 prevent informal probate of a will or informal issuance of letters for a period of five days from death. The last sentence prevents the survivorship requirement from affecting inheritances by the last eligible relative of the intestate who survives him for any period.

I.R.C. §2056(b) (3) makes it clear that an interest passing to a surviving spouse is *not* made a "terminable interest" and thereby disqualified for inclusion in the marital deduction by its being conditioned on failure of the spouse to survive a period not exceeding six months after the decedent's death, if the spouse in fact lives for the required period. Thus, the intestate share of a spouse who survives the decedent by five days is available for the marital deduction. To assure a marital deduction in cases where one spouse fails to survive the other by the required period, the decedent must leave a will. The marital deduction is not a problem in the typical intestate estate. The draftsmen and Special Committee concluded that the statute should accommodate the typical estate to which it applies, rather than the unusual case of an unplanned estate involving large sums of money.

Section 2-105. No Taker.

If there is no taker under the provisions of this Article, the intestate estate passes to the (state).

Section 2-106. Representation.

If representation is called for by this Code, the estate is divided into as many shares as there are surviving heirs in the nearest degree of kinship and deceased persons in the same degree who left issue who survive the decedent, each surviving heir in the nearest degree receiving one share and the share of each deceased person in the same degree being divided among his issue in the same manner.

COMMENT

Under the system of intestate succession in effect in some states, property is directed to be divided "per stirpes" among issue or descendants of identified ancestors. Applying a meaning commonly associated with the quoted words, the estate is first divided into the number indicated by the number of children of the ancestor who survive, *or* who leave issue who survive. If, for example, the property is directed to issue "per stirpes" of the intestate's parents, the first division would be by the number of children of parents (other than the intestate) who left issue surviving even though no person of this generation survives. Thus, if the survivors are a child and a grandchild of a deceased brother of the intestate and five children of his deceased sister, the brother's descendants would divide one-half and the five children of the sister would divide the other half. Yet, if the parent of the brother's grandchild also had survived, most statutes would give the seven nephews and nieces equal shares because it is commonly provided that if all surviving kin are in equal degree, they take per capita.

The draft rejects this pattern and keys to a system which

assures that the first and principal division of the estate will be with reference to a generation which includes one or more living members.

Section 2-107. Kindred of Half Blood.

Relatives of the half blood inherit the same share they would inherit if they were of the whole blood.

Section 2-108. Afterborn Heirs.

Relatives of the decedent conceived before his death but born thereafter inherit as if they had been born in the lifetime of the decedent.

Section 2-109. Meaning of Child and Related Terms.

If, for purposes of intestate succession, a relationship of parent and child must be established to determine succession by, through, or from a person,

(1) an adopted person is the child of an adopting parent and not of the natural parents except that adoption of a child by the spouse of a natural parent has no effect on the relationship between the child and either natural parent.

(2) In cases not covered by Paragraph (1), a person is the child of its parents regardless of the marital status of its parents and the parent and child relationship may be established under the [Uniform Parentage Act]

Alternatives subsection (2) for states that have not adopted the Uniform Parentage Act.

[(2) In cases not covered by Paragraph (1), a person born out of wedlock is a child of the mother. That person is also a child of the father, if:

(i) the natural parents participated in a marriage ceremony before or after the birth of the child, even though the attempted marriage is void; or

(ii) the paternity is established by an adjudication before the death of the father or is established thereafter by clear and convincing proof, but the paternity established under this subparagraph is ineffective to qualify the father or his kindred to inherit from or through the child unless the father has openly treated the child as his, and has not refused to support the child.]

COMMENT

The definition of "child" and "parent" in Section 1-201 incorporates the meanings established by this section, thus extending them for all purposes of the Code. See Section 2-802 for the definition of "spouse" for purposes of intestate succession.

The change in 1975 from "that" to "either" as the third from the last word in subsection (1) was recommended by the Joint Editorial Board so that children would not be detached from any natural relatives for inheritance purposes because of adoption by the spouse of one of its natural parents. The change in this section, which is referred to by the definitions in Section 1-201 of "child", "issue" and "parent", affects, inter alia, the meaning of Sections 2-102, 2-103, 2-106, 2-302, 2-401, 2-402, 2-403, 2-404, and 2-605. As one consequence, the child of a deceased father who has been adopted by the mother's new spouse does not cease to be "issue" of his father and his parents, and so, under Section 2-605, would take a devise from one of his natural, paternal grandparents in favor of the child's deceased father who predeceased the testator. This situtation is suggested by In re Estate of Bissell, 342 N.Y.S.(2d) 718.

The recommended addition of a new section, Section 2-114, dealing with the possibility of double inheritance where a person establishes relationships to a decedent through two lines of relatives is attributable, in part, to the change recommended in Section 2-109(1).

The approval in 1973 by the National Conference of Commissioners on Uniform State Laws of the Uniform Parentage Act reflects a change of policy by the Conference regarding the status of children born out of wedlock to one which is inconsistent with Section 2-109(2) of the Code as approved in 1969. The new language of 2-109(2) conforms the Uniform Probate Code to the Uniform Parentage Act. In view of the fact that eight states [as of 1975] have enacted the 1969 version of 2-109(2), the former language is retained, in brackets, to indicate that states, consistently with enactment of the Uniform Probate Code, may accept either form of approved language.

Section 2-110. Advancements.

If a person dies intestate as to all his estate, propertywhich he gave in his lifetime to an heir is treated as an advancement against the latter's share of the estate only if declared in a contemporaneous writing by the decedent or acknowledged in writing by the heir to be an advancement. For this purpose the property advanced is valued as of the time the heir came into possession or enjoyment of the property or as of the time of death of the decedent, whichever first occurs. If the recipient of the property fails to survive the decedent, the property is not taken into account in computing the intestate share to be received by the recipient's issue, unless the declaration or acknowledgment provides otherwise.

COMMENT

This section alters the common law relating to advancements by requiring written evidence of the intent that an inter vivos gift be an advancement. The statute is phrased in terms of the donee being an "heir" because the transaction is regarded as of decedent's death; of course, the donee is only a prospective heir at the time of the transfer during lifetime. Most inter vivos transfers today are intended to be absolute gifts or are carefully integrated into a total estate plan. If the donor intends that any transfer during lifetime be deducted from the donee's share of his estate, the donor may either execute a will so providing or, if he intends to die intestate, charge the gift as an advance by a writing within the present section. The present section applies only when the decedent died intestate and not when he leaves a will.

This section applies to advances to collaterals (such as nephews and nieces) as well as to lineal descendants. The statute does not spell out the method of taking account of the advance, since this process is well settled by the common law and is not a source of litigation.

Section 2-111. Debts to Decedent.

A debt owed to the decedent is not charged against the intestate share of any person except the debtor. If the debtor fails to survive the decedent, the debt is not taken into account in computing the intestate share of the debtor's issue.

Section 2-112. Alienage.

No person is disqualified to take as an heir because he or a person through whom he claims is or has been an alien.

COMMENT

The purpose of this section is to eliminate the ancient rule that an alien cannot acquire or transmit land by descent, a rule based on the feudal notions of the obligations of the tenant to the king. Although there never was a corresponding rule as to personalty, the present section is phrased in light of the basic premise of the Code that distinctions between real and personal property should be abolished.

This section has broader vitality in light of the recent decision of the United States Supreme Court in Zschernig v. Miller, 88 S.Ct. 664, 389 U.S. 429, 19 L.Ed.2d 683 (1968) holding unconstitutional a state statute providing for escheat if a nonresident alien cannot meet three requirements: the existence of a reciprocal right of a United States citizen to take property on the same terms as a citizen or inhabitant of the foreign country, the right of United States citizens to receive payment here of funds from estates in the foreign country, and the right of the foreign heirs to receive the proceeds of the local estate without confiscation by the foreign government. The rationale was that such a statute involved the local probate court in matters which essentially involve United States foreign policy, whether or not there is a governing treaty with the foreign country. Hence, the statute is "an intrusion by the State into the field of foreign affairs which the Constitution entrusts to the President and the Congress".

Section 2-113. Dower and Curtesy Abolished.

The estates of dower and curtesy are abolished.

COMMENT

The provisions of this Code replace the common law concepts of dower and curtesy and their statutory counterparts. Those estates provided both a share in intestacy and a protection against disinheritance.

In states which have previously abolished dower and curtesy, or where those estates have never existed, the above section should be omitted.

Section 2-114. Persons Related to Decedent Through Two Lines.

A person who is related to the decedent through two lines of relationship is entitled to only a single share based on the relationship which would entitle him to the larger share.

COMMENT

This section was added in 1975. The language is identical to that appearing as Section 2-112 in U.P.C. Working Drafts 3 and 4, and as Section 2-110 in Working Draft 5. The section was dropped because, with adoptions serving to transplant adopted children from all natural relationships to full relationship with adoptive relatives, and inheritance eliminated as between persons more distantly related than descendants of a common grandparent, the prospects of double inheritance seemed too remote to warrant the burden of an extra section. The changes recommended in Section 2-109(1) increase the prospects of double inheritance to the point where the addition of Section 2-114 seemed desirable. The section would have potential application in the not uncommon case where a deceased person's brother or sister marries the spouse of the decedent and adopts a child of the former marriage; it would block inheritance through two lines if the adopting parent died thereafter leaving the child as a natural and adopted grandchild of its grandparents.

PART 2

ELECTIVE SHARE OF SURVIVING SPOUSE

GENERAL COMMENT

The sections of this Part describe a system for common law states designed to protect a spouse of a decedent who was a domiciliary against donative transfers by will and will substitutes which would deprive the survivor of a "fair share" of the decedent's estate. Optional sections adapting the elective share system to community property jurisdictions were contained in preliminary drafts, but were dropped from the final Code. Problems of disinheritance of spouses in community states are limited to situations involving assets acquired by domiciliaries of common law states who later become domiciliaries of a community property state, and to instances where substantially all of a deceased spouse's property is separate property. Representatives of community property states differ in regard to whether either of these problem areas warrant statutory solution.

Almost every feature of the system described herein is or may be controversial. Some have questioned the need for any legislation checking the power of married persons to transfer their property as they please. See Plager, "The Spouse's Nonbarrable Share: A Solution in Search of a Problem", 33 Chi.L.Rev. 681 (1966). Still, all common law states except the Dakotas appear to impose some restriction on the power of a spouse to disinherit the other. In some, the ancient concept of dower continues to prevent free transfer of land by a married person. In most states, including many which have abolished dower, a spouse's protection is found in statutes which give a surviving spouse the power to take a share of the decedent's probate estate upon election rejecting the provisions of the decedent's will. These statutes expand the spouse's protection to all real and personal assets owned by the decedent at death, but usually take no account of various will substitutes which permit an owner to transfer ownership at his death without use of a will. Judicial doctrines identifying certain transfers to be "illusory"or to be in "fraud" of the spouse's share have been evolved in some jurisdictions to offset the problems caused by will substitutes, and in New York and Pennsylvania statutes have extended the elective share of a surviving spouse to certain non-testamentary transfers.

Questions relating to the proper size of a spouse's protected interest may be raised in addition to those concerning the need for, and method of assuring, any protection. The traditions in both common law and community property states point toward some capital sum related to the size of the deceased spouse's holdings rather than to the needs of the surviving spouse. The community property pattern produces one-half for the surviving spouse, but is somewhat misleading as an analogy, for it takes no account of the decedent's separate property. The fraction of one-third, which is stated in Section 2-201, has the advantage of familiarity, for it is used in many forced share statutes.

Although the system described herein may seem complex, it should not complicate administration of a married person's estate in any but very unusual cases. The surviving spouse rather than the executor or the probate court has the burden of asserting an election, as well as the burden of proving the matters which must be shown in order to make a successful claim to more than he or she has received. Some of the apparent complexity arises from Section 2-202, which has the effect of compelling an electing spouse to allow credit for all funds attributable to the decedent when the spouse, by electing, is claiming that more is due. This feature should serve to reduce the number of instances in which an elective share will be asserted. Finally, Section 2-204 expands the effectiveness of attempted waivers and releases of rights to claim an elective share. Thus, means by which estate planners can assure clients that their estates will not become embroiled in election litigation are provided.

Uniformity of law on the problems covered by this Part is much to be desired. It is especially important that states limit the applicability of rules protecting spouses so that only estates of domiciliary decedents are involved.

Section 2-201. Right to Elective Share.

(a) If a married person domiciled in this state dies, the surviving spouse has a right of election to take an elective share of one-third of the augmented estate under the limitations and conditions hereinafter stated.

(b) If a married person not domiciled in this state dies, the right, if any, of the surviving spouse to take an elective share in property in this state is governed by the law of the decedent's domicile at death.

COMMENT

Under the common law a widow was entitled to dower, which was a life estate in a fraction of lands of which her husband was seized of an estate of inheritance at any time during the marriage. Dower encumbers titles and provides inadequate protection for widows in a society which classifies most wealth as personal property. Hence the states have tended to substitute a forced share in the whole estate for dower and the widower's comparable common law right of curtesy. Few existing forced share statutes make adequate provisions for transfers by means other than succession to the surviving spouse and others. This and the following sections are designed to do so. The theory of these sections is discussed in Fratcher, "Toward Uniform Succession Legislation," 41 N.Y.U. L.Rev. 1037, 1050-1064 (1966). The existing law is discussed in MacDonald, "Fraud on the Widow's Share" (1960). Legislation comparable to that suggested here became effective in New York on Sept. 1, 1966. See Decedent Estate Law, §18.

Section 2-202. Augmented Estate.

The augmented estate means the estate reduced by funeral and administration expenses, homestead allowance, family allowances and exemptions, and enforceable claims, to which is added the sum of the following amounts:

(1)The value of property transferred by the decedent at any time during marriage, to or for the benefit of any person other than the surviving spouse, to the extent that the decedent did not receive adequate and full consideration in money or money's worth for the transfer, if the transfer is of any of the following types:

(i) any transfer under which the decedent retained at the time of his death the possession or enjoyment of, or right to income from, the property;

(ii) any transfer to the extent that the decedent retained at the time of his death a power, either alone or in conjunction with any other person, to revoke or to consume, invade or dispose of the principal for his own benefit;

(iii) any transfer whereby property is held at the time of decedent's death by decedent and another with right of survivorship;

(iv) any transfer made within two years of death of the decedent to the extent that the aggregate transfers to any one donee in either of the years exceed $3,000.

Any transfer is excluded if made with the written consent or joinder of the surviving spouse. Property is valued as of the decedent's death except that property given irrevocably to a donee during lifetime of the decedent is valued as of the date the donee came into possession or enjoyment if that occurs first. Nothing herein shall cause to be included in the augmented estate any life insurance, accident insurance, joint annuity, or pension payable to a person other than the surviving spouse.

(2) The value of property owned by the surviving spouse at the decedent's death, plus the value of property transferred by the spouse at any time during marriage to any person other than the decedent which would have been includible in the spouse's augmented estate if the surviving spouse had predeceased the decedent, to the extent the owned or transferred property is derived from the decedent by any means other than testate or intestate succession without a full consideration in money or money's worth. For purposes of this subsection:

(i) Property derived from the decedent includes, but is not limited to, any beneficial interest of the surviving spouse in a trust created by the decedent during his lifetime, any property appointed to the spouse by the decedent's exercise of a general or special power of appointment also exercisable in favor of others than the spouse, any proceeds of insurance (including accidental death benefits) on the life of the decedent attributable to premiums paid by him, any lump sum immediately payable and the commuted value of the proceeds of annuity contracts under which the decedent was the primary annuitant attributable to premiums paid by him, the commuted value of amounts payable after the decedent's death under any public or private pension, disability compensation, death benefit or retirement plan, exclusive of the Federal Social Security system, by reason of service performed or disabilities incurred by the decedent, and the value of the share of the surviving spouse resulting from rights in community property in this or any other state formerly owned with the decedent. Premiums paid by the decedent's employer, his partner, a partnership of which he was a member, or his creditors, are deemed to have been paid by the decedent.

(ii) Property owned by the spouse at the decedent's

death is valued as of the date of death. Property transferred by the spouse is valued at the time the transfer became irrevocable, or at the decedent's death, whichever occurred first. Income earned by included property prior to the decedent's death is not treated as property derived from the decedent.

(iii) Property owned by the surviving spouse as of the decedent's death, or previously transferred by the surviving spouse, is presumed to have been derived from the decedent, except to the extent that the surviving spouse establishes that it was derived from another source.

(3) For purposes of this section a bona fide purchaser is a purchaser for value in good faith and without notice of any adverse claim. Any recorded instrument on which a state documentary fee is noted pursuant to [insert appropriate reference] is prima facie evidence that the transfer described therein was made to a bona fide purchaser.

COMMENT

The purpose of the concept of augmenting the probate estate in computing the elective share is twofold: (1) to prevent the owner of wealth from making arrangements which transmit his property to others by means other than probate deliberately to defeat the right of the surviving spouse to a share, and (2) to prevent the surviving spouse from electing a share of the probate estate when the spouse has received a fair share of the total wealth of the decedent either during the lifetime of the decedent or at death by life insurance, joint tenancy assets and other nonprobate arrangements. Thus essentially two separate groups of property are added to the net probate estate to arrive at the augmented net estate which is the basis for computing the one-third share of the surviving spouse. In the first category are transfers by the decedent during his lifetime which are essentially will substitutes, arrangements which give him continued benefits or controls over the property. However, only transfers during the marriage are included in this category. This makes it possible for a person to provide for children by a prior marriage, as by a revocable living trust, without concern that such provisions will be upset by later marriage. The limitation to transfers during marriage reflects some of the policy underlying community property. What kinds of transfers should be included here is a matter of reasonable difference of opinion. The finespun tests of the Federal Estate Tax Law might be utilized, of course. However, the objectives of a tax law are different from those involved here in the Probate Code, and the present section is therefore more limited. It is intended to reach the kinds of transfers readily usable to defeat an elective share in only the probate estate.

In the second category of assets, property of the surviving spouse derived from the decedent and property derived from the decedent which the spouse has, in turn, given away in a transaction that is will-like in effect or purpose, the scope is much broader. Thus a person can during his lifetime make outright gifts to relatives and they are not included in this first category unless they are made within two years of death (the exception being designed to prevent a person from depleting his estate in contemplation of death). But the time when the surviving spouse derives her wealth from the decedent is immaterial; thus if a husband has purchased a home in the wife's name and made systematic gifts to the wife over many years, the home and accumulated wealth she owns at his death as a result of such gifts ought to, and under this section do, reduce her share of the augmented estate. Likewise, for policy reasons, life insurance is not included in the first category of transfers to other persons, because it is not ordinarily purchased as a way of depleting the probate estate and avoiding the elective share of the spouse; but life insurance proceeds payable to the surviving spouse are included in the second category, because it seems unfair to allow a surviving spouse to disturb the decedent's estate plan if the spouse has received ample provision from life insurance. In this category no distinction is drawn as to whether the transfers are made before or after marriage.

Depending on the circumstances it is obvious that this section will operate in the long run to decrease substantially the number of elections. This is because the statute will encourage and provide a legal base for counseling of testators against schemes to disinherit the spouse, and because the spouse can no longer elect in cases where substantial provision is made by joint tenancy, life insurance, lifetime gifts, living trusts set up by the decedent, and the other numerous nonprobate arrangements by which wealth is today transferred. On the other hand the section should provide realistic protection against disinheritance of the spouse in the rare case where decedent tries to achieve that purpose by depleting his probate estate.

The augmented net estate approach embodied in this section is relatively complex and assumes that litigation may be required in cases in which the right to an elective share is asserted. The proposed scheme should not complicate administration in well-planned or routine cases, however, because the spouse's rights are freely releasable under Section 2-204 and because of the time limits in Section 2-205. Some legislatures may wish to consider a simpler approach along the lines of the Pennsylvania Estates Act provision reading:

"A conveyance of assets by a person who retains a power of appointment by will, or a power of revocation or consumption over the principal thereof, shall at the election of his surviving spouse, be treated as a testamentary disposition so far as the surviving spouse is concerned to the extent to which the power has been reserved, but the right of the surviving spouse shall be subject to the rights of any income beneficiary whose interest in income becomes vested in enjoyment prior to the death of the conveyor. The provisions of this subsection shall not apply to any contract of life insurance purchased by a decedent, whether payable in trust orotherwise."

In passing, it is to be noted that a Pennsylvania widow apparently may claim against a revocable trust or will even though she has been amply provided for by life insurance or other means arranged by the decedent. Penn. Stats. Annot. title 20, §301.11(a).

The New York Estates, Powers and Trusts Law §5-1.1 (b) also may be suggested as a model. It treats as testamentary dispositions all gifts causa mortis, money on deposit by the decedent in trust for another, money deposited in the decedent's name payable on death to another, joint tenancy property, and transfers by decedent over which he has a power to revoke or invade. The New York law also expressly excludes life insurance, pension plans, and United States savings bonds payable to a designated person. One of the drawbacks of the New York legislation is its complexity, much of which is attributable to the effort to prevent a spouse from taking an elective share when the deceased spouse has followed certain prescribed procedures. The scheme described by Sections 2-201 et seq. of this draft, like that of all states except New York, leaves the question of whether a spouse may or may not elect to be controlled by the economics of the situation, rather than by conditions on the statutory right. Further, the New York system gives the spouse election rights in spite of the possibility that the spouse has been well provided for by insurance or other gifts from the decedent.

In 1975, the Joint Editorial Board recommended the addition of reference to bona fide purchaser in paragraph (1), "to a donee" in paragraph (1)(iv) and the addition of paragraph (3) to the above section to reflect recommendations evolved in discussions by committees of the Colorado Bar Association to meet title problems that had been identified under the Code as originally enacted. One problem that should be cured by the amendments rose when real property experts in Colorado took the position that, since any transfer might be found to be for less than "adequate and full consideration in money or money's worth," the language of the original text, all deeds from married persons had to be jointed in by the spouse, lest the grantor die within two years and the grantee be subjected to the claim that the value involved was a part of the augmented estate.

Also, the Joint Editorial Board in 1975 recommended the addition in Section 2-202(2)(i) of language referring to property moving to the surviving spouse via joint and survivorship holdings with the decedent. The addition would not, in all probability, change the meaning of the subsection, but it would clarify it in relation to jointly held property which will be present in a great number of cases.

Section 2-203. Right of Election Personal to Surviving Spouse.

The right of election of the surviving spouse may be exercised only during his lifetime by him. In the case of a protected person, the right of election may be exercised only by order of the court in which protective proceedings as to his property are pending, after finding that exercise is necessary to provide adequate support for the protected person during his probable life expectancy.

Section 2-204. Waiver of Right to Elect and of Other Rights.

The right of election of a surviving spouse and the rights of the surviving spouse to homestead allowance, exempt property and family allowance, or any of them, may be waived, wholly or partially, before or after marriage, by a written contract, agreement or waiver signed by the party waiving after fair disclosure. Unless it provides to the contrary, a waiver of "all rights" (or equivalent language) in the property or estate of a present or prospective spouse or a complete property settlement entered into after or in anticipation of separation or divorce is a waiver of all rights to elective share, homestead allowance, exempt property, and family allowance by each spouse in the property of the other and a renunciation by each of all benefits which would otherwise pass to him from the other by intestate succession or by virtue of the provisions of any will executed before the waiver or property settlement.

COMMENT

The right to homestead allowance is conferred by Section 2-401, that to exempt property by Section 2-402, and that to family allowance by Section 2-403. The right to renounce interests passing by testate or intestate succession is recognized by Section 2-801. The provisions of this section, permitting a spouse or prospective spouse to waive all statutory rights in the other spouse's property seem desirable in view of the common and commendable desire of parties to second and later marriages to insure that property derived from prior spouses passes at death to the issue of the prior spouses instead of to the newly acquired spouse. The operation of a property settlement as a waiver and renunication takes care of the situation which arises when a spouse dies while a divorce suit is pending.

Section 2-205. Proceeding for Elective Share; Time Limit.

(a) The surviving spouse may elect to take his elective share in the augmented estate by filing in the Court and mailing or delivering to the personal representative, if any, a petition for the elective share within nine months after the date of death, or within six months after the probate of the decedent's Will, whichever limitation last expires. However, non-probate transfers, described in Section 2-202(1), shall not be included within the augmented estate for the purpose of computing the elective share, if the petition is filed later than nine months after death.

The Court may extend the time for election as it sees fit for cause shown by the surviving spouse before the time for election has expired.

(b) The surviving spouse shall give notice of the time and place set for hearing to persons interested in the estate and to the distributees and recipients of portions of the augmented net estate whose interests will be adversely affected by the taking of the elective share.

(c) The surviving spouse may withdraw his demand for an elective share at any time before entry of a final determination by the court.

(d) After notice and hearing, the court shall determine the amount of the elective share and shall order its payment from the assets of the augmented net estate or by contribution as appears appropriate under Section 2-207. If it appears that a fund or property included in the augmented net estate has not come into the possession of the personal representative, or has been distributed by the personal representative, the court nevertheless shall fix the liability of any person who has any interest in the fund or property or who has possession thereof, whether as trustee or otherwise. The proceeding may be maintained against fewer than all persons against whom relief could be sought, but no person is subject to contribution in any greater amount than he would have been if relief had been secured against all persons subject to contribution.

(e) The order or judgment of the court may be enforced as necessary in suit for contribution or payment in other courts of this state or other jurisdictions.

COMMENT

In 1975, the Joint Editorial Board recommended changes in subsection (a) that were designed to meet a question, arising under the original text, of whether the right to an elective share was ever barred in cases of unadministered estates. The new language also has the effect of clearing included, non-probate transfers to persons other than the surviving spouse of the lien of any possible elective share proceeding unless the spouse's action is commenced within nine months after death. This bar on efforts to recapture non-probate assets for an elective share does not apply to probate assets. Probate assets may be controlled by a Will that may not be offered for probate until as late as three years from death. As to these, the limitation on the surviving spouse's proceeding is six months after the probate.

Section 2-206. Effect of Election on Benefits by Will or Statute.

A surviving spouse is entitled to homestead allowance, exempt property, and family allowance, whether or not he elects to take an elective share.

COMMENT

The election does not result in a loss of benefits under the Will (in the absence of renunciation) because those benefits are charged against the elective share under Sections 2-201, 2-202, and 2-207(a).

In 1975, the Joint Editorial Board recommended changes in this and the following section that reverse the position of the original text which permitted an electing spouse to accept or reject particular benefits as provided him by the decedent without reducing the dollar value of his elective share. The new language in this section, replacing former Section 2-206(a) and (b), does not mention renunciation of transfers which is now dealt with in Section 2-207. The remaining content of this section is restricted to a simple statement indicating that the family exemptions described by Article II, Part 4 may be distributed from the probate estate without reference to whether an elective share right is asserted, and without being charged to the electing spouse as a part of the elective share. In the view of the Board, deletion of language in the original form of Section 2-206(b), dealing with devises that are intended to be in lieu of family exemptions, does not alter the ability of a testator, by express provision in the Will, from putting a surviving spouse to an election between accepting the devises provided or accepting the family exemptions provided by law. This matter is dealt with in Sections 2-401, 2-402, 2-403 and 2-404.

Section 2-207. Charging Spouse With Gifts Received; Liability of Others For Balance of Elective Share.

(a) In the proceeding for an elective share, property which is part of the augmented estate which passes or has passed to the surviving spouse by testate or intestate succession or other means and which has not been renounced, including that described in Section 2-202(3), is applied first to satisfy the elective share and to reduce the amount due from other recipients of portions of the augmented estate.

(b) Remaining property of the augmented estate is so applied that liability for the balance of the elective share of the surviving spouse is equitably apportioned among the recipients of the augmented estate in proportion to the value of their interests therein.

(c) Only original transferees from, or appointees of, the decedent and their donees, to the extent the donees have the property or its proceeds, are subject to the contribution to make up the elective share of the surviving spouse. A person liable to contribution may choose to give up the property transferred to him or to pay its value as of the time it is considered in computing the augmented estate.

COMMENT

Sections 2-401, 2-402 and 2-403 have the effect of giving a spouse certain exempt property and allowances in addition to the amount of the elective share.

In 1975, the Joint Editorial Board recommended changes in Section 2-206 and subsection (a) of this section which have the effect of protecting a decedent's plan as far as it provides values for the surviving spouse. The spouse is not compelled to accept the benefits devised by the decedent, but if these benefits are rejected, the values involved are charged to the electing spouse as if the devises were accepted. The second sentence of new subsection (a) provides a rebuttable presumption of the value of a life estate or an interest in a trust, when this form of benefit is provided for an electing spouse by the decedent's plan.

PART 3

SPOUSE AND CHILDREN UNPROVIDED FOR IN WILLS

Section 2-301. Omitted Spouse.

(a) If a testator fails to provide by will for his surviving spouse who married the testator after the execution of the will, the omitted spouse shall receive the same share of the estate he would have received if the decedent left no will unless it appears from the will that the omission was intentional or the testator provided for the spouse by transfer outside the will and the intent that the transfer be in lieu of a testamentary provision is shown by statements of the testator or from the amount of the transfer or other evidence.

(b) In satisfying a share provided by this section, the devises made by the will abate as provided in Section 3-902.

COMMENT

Section 2-508 provides that a Will not revoked by a change of circumstances occurring subsequent to is execution other than as described by that section. This section reflects the view that the intestate share of the spouse is what the decedent would want the spouse to have if he had thought about the relationship of his old Will to the new situation. One effect of this section should be to reduce the number of instances where a spouse will claim an elective share.

Section 2-302. Pretermitted Children.

(a) If a testator fails to provide in his will for any of his children born or adopted after the execution of his will, the omitted child receives a share in the estate equal in value to that which he would have received if the testator had died intestate unless:

(1) it appears from the will that the omission was intentional;

(2) when the will was executed the testator had one or more children and devised substantially all his estate to the other parent of the omitted child; or

(3) the testator provided for the child by transfer outside the will and the intent that the transfer be in lieu of a testamentary provision is shown by statements of the testator or from the amount of the transfer or other evidence.

(b) If at the time of execution of the will the testator fails to provide in his will for a living child solely because he believes the child to be dead, the child receives a share in the estate equal in value to that which he would have received if the testator had died intestate.

(c) In satisfying a share provided by this section, the devises made by the will abate as provided in Section 3-902.

COMMENT

This section provides for both the case where a child was born or adopted after the execution of the will and not foreseen at the time and thus not provided for in the will, and the rare case where a testator omits one of his existing children because of mistaken belief that the child is dead.

Although the sections dealing with advancement and ademption by satisfaction (2-110 and 2-612) provide that a gift during lifetime is not an advancement or satisfaction unless the testator's intent is evidenced in writing, this section permits oral evidence to establish a testator's intent that lifetime gifts or nonprobate transfers such as life insurance or joint accounts are in lieu of a testamentary provision for a child born or adopted after the will. Here there is no real contradiction of testamentary intent, since there is no provision in the will itself for the omitted child.

To preclude operation of this section it is not necessary to make any provision, even nominal in amount, for a testator's present or future children; a simple recital in the will that the testator intends to make no provision for then living children or any the testator thereafter may have would meet the requirement of (a)(1).

Under subsection (c) and Section 3-902, any intestate estate would first be applied to satisfy the share of a pretermitted child.

This section is not intended to alter the rules of evidence applicable to statements of a decedent.

PART 4

EXEMPT PROPERTY AND ALLOWANCES

GENERAL COMMENT

This part describes certain rights and values to which a surviving spouse and certain children of a deceased *domiciliary* are entitled in preference over unsecured creditors of the estate may be devised by Will. If there is a surviving spouse, all of the values described in this Part, which total $8,500 plus whatever is allowed to the spouse for support during administration, pass to the spouse. Minor or dependent children become entitled to the homestead exemption of $5,000 and to support allowances if there is no spouse, and may receive some of the support allowance if they live apart from the surviving spouse. The exempt property section confers rights on the spouse, if any, or on all children, to $3,500 in certain chattels, or funds if the unencumbered value of chattels is below the $3,500 level. This provision is designed in part to relieve a personal representative of the duty to sell household chattels when there are children who will have them.

These family protection provisions supply the basis for the important small estate provisions of Article III, Part 12.

States adopting the Code may see fit to alter the dollar amounts suggested in these sections, or to vary the terms and conditions in other ways so as to accommodate existing traditions. Although creditors of estates would be aided somewhat if all family exemption provisionss relating to probate estates were the same throughout the country, there is probably less need for uniformity of law regarding these provisions than for any of the other parts of this article. Still, it is quite important for all states to limit their homestead, support allowance and exempt property provisions, if any, so that they apply only to estates of decedents who were domiciliaries of the state.

Notice that Section 2-104 imposes a requirement of survival of the decedent for 120 hours on any spouse or child claiming under this Part.

Section 2-401. Homestead Allowance.

A surviving spouse of a decedent who was domiciled in this state is entitled to a homestead allowance of [$5,000]. If there is no surviving spouse, each minor child and each dependent child of the decedent is entitled to a homestead allowance amounting to [$5,000] divided by the number of minor and dependent children of the decedent. The homestead allowance is exempt from and has priority over all claims against the estate. Homestead allowance is in addition to any share passing to the surviving spouse or minor or dependent child by the Will of the decedent unless otherwise provided, by intestate succession or by way of elective share.

COMMENT

See Section 2-802 for the definition of "spouse" which controls in this Part. Also, see Section 2-104. Waiver of homestead is covered by Section 2-204. "Election" between a provision of a Will and homestead is not required unless the Will so provides.

A set dollar amount for homestead allowance was dictated by the desirability of having a certain level below which administration may be dispensed with or be handled summarily, without regard to the size of allowances under Section 2-402. The "small estate" line is controlled largely, though not entirely by the size of the homestead allowance. This is because Part 12 of Article III dealing with small estates rests on the assumption that the only justification for keeping a decedent's assets from his creditors is to benefit the decedent's spouse and children.

Another reason for a set amount is related to the fact that homestead allowance may prefer a decedent's minor or dependent children over his other children. It was felt desirable to minimize the consequence of application of an arbitrary age line among children of the testator.

Section 2-401A. Constitutional Homestead.

The value of any constitutional right of homestead in the family home received by a surviving spouse or child shall be charged against that spouse or child's homestead allowance to the extens that the family home is part of the decedent's estate or would have been but for the homestead provision of the constitution.

COMMENT

This optional section is designed for adoption only in states with a constitutional homestead provision. The value of the surviving spouse's constitutional right of homestead may be considerably less than the full value of the family home if the constitution gives her only a terminable life estate enjoyable in common with minor children.

Section 2-402. Exempt Property.

In addition to the homestead allowance, the surviving spouse of a decedent who was domiciled in this state is entitled from the estate to a value not exceeding $3,500 in excess of any security interests therein in household furniture, automobiles, furnishings, appliances and personal effects. If there is no survivng spouse, children of the decedent are entitled jointly to the same value. If encumbered chattels are selected and if the value in excess of security interests, plus that of other exempt property, is less than $3,500 or if there is not $3,500 worth of exempt property in the estate, the spouse or children are entitled to other assets of the estate, if any, to the extent necessary to make up the $3,500 value. Rights to exempt property and assets needed to make up a deficiency of exempt property have priority over all claims against the estate, except that the right to any assets to make up a deficiency of exempt property shall abate as necessary to permit prior payment of homestead allowance and family allowance. These rights are in addition to any benefit or share passing to the surviving spouse or children by the Will of the decedent unless otherwise provided, by intestate succession, or by way of elective share.

COMMENT

Unlike the exempt values described in Sections 2-401 and 2-403, the exempt values described in this section are available in a case where the decedent left no spouse but left only adult children. The possible difference between beneficiaries of the exemptions described by Sections 2-401 and 2-403, and this section, explain the provision in this section which establishes priorities.

Section 2-204 covers waiver of exempt property rights. This section indicates that a decedent's Will may put a spouse to an election with reference to exemptions, but that no election is presumed to be required.

Section 2-403. Family Allowance.

In addition to the right to homestead allowance and exempt property, if the decedent was domiciled in this state, the surviving sposue and minor children whom the decedent was obligated to support and children who were in fact being supported by him are entitled to a reasonable allowance in money out of the estate for their maintenance during the period of administration, which allowance may not continue for longer than one year if the estate is inadequate to discharge allowed claims. The allowance may be paid as a lump sum or in periodic installments. It is payable to the surviving spouse, if living, for the use of the surviving spouse and minor and dependent children; otherwise to the children, or persons having their care and custody; but in case any minor child or dependent child is not living with the surviving spouse, the allowance may be made partially to the child or his guardian or other person having his care and custody, and partially to the spouse, as their needs may appear. The family allowance is exempt from and has priority over all claims but not over the homestead allowance.

The family allowance in not chargeable against any benefit or share passing to the surviving spouse or children by the Will of the decedent unless otherwise provided, by intestate succession, or by way of elective share. The death of any person entitled to family allowance terminates his right to allowances not yet paid.

COMMENT

The allowance provided by this section does not qualify for the marital deduction under the Federal Estate Tax Act because the interest is terminable. A broad code must be drafted to provide the best possible protection for the family in all cases, even though this may not provide desired tax advantage for certain larger estates. In the estates falling in the federal estate tax bracket where careful planning may be expected, it is important to the operation of formula clauses that the family allowance be clearly terminable or clearly nonterminable. With the proposed section clearly creating a terminable interest, estate planners can create a plan which will operate with certainty. Finally, in order to facilitate administration of this allowance without court supervision it is necessary to provide a fairly simple and definite framework.

In determining the amount of the family allowance, account should be taken of both the previous standard of living and the nature of other resources available to the family to meet current living expenses until the estate can be administered and assets distributed. While the death of the principal income producer may necessitate some change in the standard of living, there must also be a period of adjustment. If the surviving spouse has a substantial income, this may be taken into account. Whether life insurance proceeds payable in a lump sum or periodic installments were intended by the decedent to be used for the period of adjustment or to be conserved as capital may be considered. A living trust may provide the needed income without resorting to the probate estate. If a husband has been the principal source of family support, a wife should not be expected to use her capital to support the family.

Obviously, need is relative to the circumstances, and what is reasonable must be decided on the basis of the facts of each individual case. Note, however, that under the next section the personal representative may not determine an allowance of more than $500 per month for one year; a Court order would be necessary if a greater allowance is reasonably necessary.

Section 2-104. Source, Determination and Documentation.

If the estate is otherwise sufficient, property specifically devised is not used to satisfy rights to homestead and exempt property. Subject to this restriction, the surviving spouse, the guardians of the minor children, or children who are adults may select property of the estate as homestead allowance and exempt property. The personal representative may make these selections if the surviving spouse, the children or the guardians of the minor children are unable or fail to do so within a reasonable time or if there are no guardians of the minor children. The personal representative may execute an instrument or deed of distribution to establish ownership of property taken as homestead allowance or exempt property. He may determine the family allowance in a lump sum not exceeding $6,000 or periodic installments not exceeding $500 per month for one year, and may disburse funds of the estate in payment of the family allowance and any part of the homestead allowance payable in cash. The personal representative or any interested person aggrieved by any selection, determination, payment, proposed payment, or failure to act under this section may petition the Court for appropriate relief, which relief may provide a family allowance larger or smaller than that which the personal representative determined or could have determined.

Chapter 10

ADMINISTRATION OF THE ESTATE

IN GENERAL—

When the decedent dies intestate, it is usually necessary that an administrator or administratrix be appointed to administer the estate. Whenever the estate is indebted, administration is usually necessary; however, where the decedent leaves only exempt property which passes to the surviving spouse, or only leaves one person entitled to distribution as sole heir, administration is generally not necessary.

APPOINTMENT OF ADMINISTRATOR—

The person primarily entitled to inherit is usually appointed administrator. The statutes designating the order of preference of appointment follow the order of inheritance. In appointment of an administrator, preference is usually granted in the following order: 1. surviving husband or wife; 2. children; 3. grandchildren; 4. father or mother; 5. brother or sister; 6. others entitled to share in the distribution of the estate. A creditor of the estate may qualify as administrator if the decedent left no next of kin. The court will usually appoint the Public Administrator to administer the estate, if no next of kin can be found. In some states his right to appointment is prior to that of creditors.

Persons under twenty-one years of age, persons convicted of a felony, and aliens who are not residents of the state are disqualified to act as administrators. Statutes usually also prohibit illiterate persons, adjudicated incompetents and persons hostile to or adversely interested in the estate from acting as administrators.

A petition must be filed by the applicant for appointment and notice is then given to all persons who have an interest in the disposition of the estate. The surrogate or probate judge may order a hearing, following which he will render a decision granting or refusing the Letters of Administration. The administrator is usually required to post a bond to insure the faithful performance of the duties of his office.

ESTATE MANAGEMENT

On appointment, the first duty of the administrator is to collect the decedent's assets. He will also prepare a full inventory of all property which comes into his possession. The administrator has the power and is under a duty to collect all debts which were owed to the decedent, and bring action against the debtor, if necessary. Usually, an administrator may not continue a decedent's business, and if he does so, he becomes chargeable with all losses incurred and profits made.

The administrator must also ascertain and pay all debts and claims against the decedent's estate. The statutes frequently allow the administrator to give notice to creditors that they present their claims within a certain period of time; if no claim is made within that time the creditor is barred from asserting it at a later date.

In order to take possession of certain assets, it may be necessary to obtain a waiver from the State Tax Department. Before a bank or trust company will transfer the decedent's account to the administrator, the bank will usually require that the administrator present a tax waiver together with a certified copy of the Letters of Administration.

Upon collection of all of the assets, the administrator will file an inventory with the State Tax Commission, and an appraiser will be appointed. After the appraisal of the estate is completed, the surrogate or probate judge will sign an order fixing the estate tax. The administrator, however, need not wait until the order is signed before paying the estate tax; payment may be made immediately or at any time before it is due, whereupon the estate will then be entitled to a discount.

The estate may also be liable for a Federal Estate Tax, which is determined by the Internal Revenue Service. The determination in the state tax proceeding is not necessarily conclusive as to value of the estate, as affected by provisions of the Federal Tax law.

Due to the complexities that may arise in the administration and management of the estate, the administrator should retain an attorney to properly advise him of his legal rights, duties and liabilities.

After the payments of taxes and debts, the administrator will distribute to the distributees their share of the estate, as determined by the inheritance laws. Any dispute as to the amount or share received by any beneficiary is decided by the surrogate or probate court. After the administrator has made his distributions, his next duty is to file an accounting with the court.

ESTATE ACCOUNTING

The administrator is obliged, on the accounting proceeding, to account for all of his actions while serving in a fiduciary capacity. All persons having an interest in the disposition of the estate must be given notice of the proceeding, and will be required to show the court some valid reason why the account should not be accepted and why the administrator should not be discharged from any further responsibility. If a relative of the decedent objects to the disposition of the estate, or if a creditor of the estate contends that he was not paid, an objection may be made at the accounting whereupon the surrogate or probate judge will grant a hearing, to determine the rights of the parties involved. An administrator must always act with a high degree of care, as he may be held personally responsible for any breach of duty, which causes a loss to the estate.

The court will sign a decree discharging the administrator from further responsibility, and granting him his commission for acting as administrator. The compensation which he receives from his services, is determined in accordance with the rates set forth in the statute. If there was any breach of the administrator's duty, due to an improper expenditure or unauthorized distribution, the surrogate will direct that a proper distribution be made and hold the administrator liable for any loss incurred.

If all persons who are interested in the disposition of the estate agree, it is possible to dispense with the accounting proceeding. The court will sign the decree and dispense with a hearing, if all distributees and creditors sign waivers of their right to object.

THE ADMINISTRATION OF SMALL ESTATES

Some states have statutes providing for simplified or no administration of small estates. The states are divided into those which permit settlement of small estates without administration or court order, those which provide for summary administration by a public official, those with provisions for simplified administration or distribution by court order, and those with provisions for collection of particular assets without administration. The state laws which provide for the collection of particular assets without administration are really exemption statutes, proving that when the estate does not exceed a certain amount, it may be set off to the widow or spouse and minor children after certain expenses are paid.[1]

---

1 A comprehensive study of state statutes which provide for simplified administration of estates was made by the New York State Law RevisionCommission. N.Y. Legis. Doc. 65(m) 1951.

TABLE OF STATUTORY REFERENCES

All citations are to the following statutory compilations as amended.

ALABAMA - Code, 1975

ALASKA - Statutes 1962

ARIZONA - Revised Statutes

ARKANSAS - Statutes, 1947

CALIFORNIA - West's Annotated Codes

COLORADO - Probate Code

CONNECTICUT - General Statutes, 1958

DELAWARE - Code, 1953

DISTRICT OF COLUMBIA - CODE, 1981

FLORIDA - Statutes

GEORGIA - Official code 1981

HAWAII - Revised Statutes

IDAHO - Code, 1949

ILLINOIS - Annotated Statutes

INDIANA - Code, 1971

KANSAS - Statutes Annotated

KENTUCKY - Revised Statutes

LOUISIANA - Revised Civil Code

MAINE - Revised Statutes, 1964

MARYLAND - Annotated Code, 1957

MASSACHUSETTS - General Laws

MICHIGAN - Compiled Laws Annotated

MINNESOTA - Statutes, 1978

MISSISSIPPI - Code, 1972

MISSOURI - Revised Statutes

MONTANA - Revised Code, 1979

NEBRASKA - Revised Statutes, 1943

NEVADA - Revised Statutes

NEW HAMPSHIRE - Revised Statutes Annotated, 1955

NEW JERSEY - Statutes Annotated

NEW MEXICO - Statutes, 1978

NEW YORK - Consolidated Laws

NORTH CAROLINA - General Statutes

NORTH DAKOTA - Century Code

OHIO - Revised Code, 1953

OKLAHOMA - Statutes, 1971

OREGON - Revised Statutes

PENNSYLVANIA - Purdons Statutes Annotated

RHODE ISLAND - General Laws, 1956

SOUTH CAROLINA - Code, 1976

SOUTH DAKOTA - Compiled Laws, 1967

TENNESSEE - Code Annotated

TEXAS - Probate Code

UTAH - Code Annotated, 1953

VERMONT - Statutes Annotated

VIRGINIA - Code, 1950

WASHINGTON - Revised Code

WEST VIRGINIA - Code

WISCONSIN - Statutes

WYOMING - Statutes, 1977

INDEX